'An amazing combination of the most sophisticated, technically documented and profound psychoanalytic reflection on music, with a "musical" and sensitive description of psychoanalytic concepts and processes. By far the most advanced exploration today in this specific area, based on the author's high expertise in both fields.'

Stefano Bolognini, *Past President of the International Psychoanalytical Association*

The Sound of the Unconscious

In this book, Ludovica Grassi explores the importance of music in psychoanalysis, arguing that music is a basic working tool for psyche, as words are composed of sound, rhythm and intonation more than lexical meaning.

Starting from ethnomusicological, evolutionary, neurodevelopmental, psychological and psychoanalytical perspectives, the book explores music's symbolic status, structure and way of operating compared to unconscious psychic functioning. Extraordinary similarities are revealed, especially in mechanisms such as repetition, imitation, variation (transformation), intimacy and the work of mourning, of the negative and of nostalgia. Moreover, silence and absence are essential components of music as well as of psychic and symbolic functioning. Time and temporality are specifically investigated in the book as key elements both in music and in symbolization and subjectivation processes. The role of the word's phonic kernel and of the voice as fundamental links to emotions, the body, the sexual and the infantile has promising implications for psychoanalytic work. All these elements find an articulation in the natural as well as complex activity of listening, which conveys a tri-dimensional and polyphonic dimension of the world, so important both in music and in psychoanalysis.

Illuminating the link between music and analysis in new and contemporary ways, *The Sound of the Unconscious* explores the resulting advances in theory and clinical practice and will be of great interest to practicing and training psychoanalysts and psychotherapists.

Ludovica Grassi, MD, is a Child Neuropsychiatrist, Full Member of the Italian Society of Psychoanalysis and IPA, Expert in Child and Adolescent Psychoanalysis and Couple and Family Psychoanalyst. Her research and publication main topics are: ethnopsychoanalysis; music and psychoanalysis; the origins of psychic life and psychoanalytic work with infants, children, adults, couples and families.

Psychoanalytic Ideas and Applications Series
IPA Publications Committee

Gabriela Legorreta (Montreal), Chair and Series Editor; Dominique Scarfone (Montreal); Catalina Bronstein (London); Lawrence Brown (Boston); Michele Ain (Montevideo); Carlos Moguillanski (Buenos Aires); Udo Hock (Berlin); Christine Kirchhoff (Berlin); Gennaro Saragnano (Rome) Consultant; Rhoda Bawdekar (London), Ex-officio as IPA Publishing Manager; Paul Crake (London), Ex-officio as IPA Executive Director

Recent titles in the series include

Permanent Disquiet
Psychoanalysis and the Transitional Subject
Michel de M'Uzan

Psychoanalytic Work with Families and Couples
Clinical Perspectives on Suffering
Susana Kuras Mauer, Sara Moscona, and Silvia Resnizky

Narcissistic Fantasies in Film and Fiction
Masters of the Universe
Ilany Kogan

Psychoanalytic Reflections on Writing, Cinema and the Arts
Facing Beauty and Loss
Paola Golinelli

Change Through Time in Psychoanalysis
Transformations and Interventions, The Three Level Model
Margaret Ann Fitzpatrick Hanly, Marina Altmann de Litvan, Ricardo Bernardi

The Sound of the Unconscious

Psychoanalysis as Music

Ludovica Grassi

LONDON AND NEW YORK

First published 2021
by Routledge
2 Park Square, Milton Park, Abingdon, Oxon OX14 4RN

and by Routledge
605 Third Avenue, New York, NY 10158

Routledge is an imprint of the Taylor & Francis Group, an informa business

© 2021 Ludovica Grassi

The right of Ludovica Grassi to be identified as author of this work has been asserted by her in accordance with sections 77 and 78 of the Copyright, Designs and Patents Act 1988.

All rights reserved. No part of this book may be reprinted or reproduced or utilised in any form or by any electronic, mechanical, or other means, now known or hereafter invented, including photocopying and recording, or in any information storage or retrieval system, without permission in writing from the publishers.

Trademark notice: Product or corporate names may be trademarks or registered trademarks, and are used only for identification and explanation without intent to infringe.

Library of Congress Cataloging-in-Publication Data
Names: Grassi, Ludovica, 1955- author.
Title: The sound of the unconscious : psychoanalysis as music / Ludovica Grassi.
Description: New York : Routledge, 2021. | Series: The International Psychoanalytical Association psychoanalytic ideas and applications series | Includes bibliographical references and index. |
Identifiers: LCCN 2020054375 (print) | LCCN 2020054376 (ebook) | ISBN 9780367645526 (hardback) | ISBN 9780367645533 (paperback) | ISBN 9781003125075 (ebook)
Subjects: LCSH: Psychoanalysis and music. | Music--Psychological aspects.
Classification: LCC ML3838 .G73 2021 (print) | LCC ML3838 (ebook) | DDC 781.1/1--dc23
LC record available at https://lccn.loc.gov/2020054375
LC ebook record available at https://lccn.loc.gov/2020054376

ISBN: 978-0-367-64552-6 (hbk)
ISBN: 978-0-367-64553-3 (pbk)
ISBN: 978-1-003-12507-5 (ebk)

Typeset in Palatino
by MPS Limited, Dehradun

First the music, then the words.*
Antonio Salieri (1786)

Note

* *Prima la musica e poi le parole,* or *First the Music, then the Words*, is the title of a one-act opera staged for the first time on 7 February 1786 in Vienna, with music by Antonio Salieri and libretto by Giovanni Battista Casti.

Contents

Acknowledgements		xi
Series Editor's Foreword		xii
Foreword		xiv
	Introduction	1
1	Sound and rhythm in psychic life and psychoanalytic work	7
2	Listening to the link: Music and primal relationships	26
3	*On imitation*	41
4	*The music is not in the notes…* Intimacy and the negative in music	59
5	Beyond space, time	71
6	Musical dialogues: The baby in a world of sound and rhythm	86
7	The musical unconscious in the family	97
8	Silence and absence: Sound and music during the coronavirus pandemic	110

Afterword	119
References	124
Index	132

Acknowledgements

I would like to thank my music teachers, and particularly Pina Buonomo and Roberto Daina, for their enthusiastic and tenacious guidance through the world of music, which sowed the seeds for my passionate relationship with it.

I would also like to express my sincere gratitude to Harriet Wolfe, who generously offered me encouragement and useful critique throughout the writing of this book, as well as to Anna Nicolò, a dear friend and colleague, who always expressed her curiosity and support for my research.

Without the careful copy-editing by Harriet Graham on my non-native English, this book would not have been so readable.

Finally, I wish to thank my son Carlo, who inspired my first steps in this research and then helped me to assemble the figures, as well as my husband Alfredo, who always read and helpfully commented my drafts.

Series Editor's Foreword

The Publications Committee of the International Psychoanalytic Association continues, with this volume, the series 'Psychoanalytic Ideas and Applications'.

The aim of this series is to focus on the scientific production of significant authors, whose works are outstanding contributions to the development of the psychoanalytic field and to set out relevant ideas and themes, generated during the history of psychoanalysis, that deserve to be known and discussed by present psychoanalysts. The relationship between psychoanalytic ideas and their applications has to be put forward from the perspective of theory, clinical practice and research, so as to maintain their validity for contemporary psychoanalysis.

The Publication's Committee's objective is to share these ideas with the psychoanalytic community and with professionals in other related disciplines, in order to expand their knowledge and generate a productive interchange between the text and the reader.

The IPA Publications Committee is pleased to publish the book *The Sound of the Unconscious: Psychoanalysis as Music* by Ludovica Grassi. The author is interested in going beyond the application of psychoanalysis to music. She proposes a musically informed psychoanalysis.

This book is a much-welcomed creative study of the omnipresent existence of sound, rhythm and music in human experience since prenatal existence. Before birth the foetus inhabits a world of sounds: sounds of blood flow, body fluid, heartbeat, movement and breath. For the author, these are the somatic-psychic foundation of human experience. Based on evidence that music is a basic working tool for the psyche as it uses the same process and mechanisms, Dr. Grassi puts forward the idea that music plays a possible role in the development and functioning of psychic life.

Dr. Grassi's ability to draw parallels between the way music and the psyche function has the potential of enlarging the range of perceivable clinical elements in the psychoanalytic encounter which in turn widens the possibilities for intervention. The psychoanalyst's attentiveness to musical components of psychic functioning carries the potential of enriching one's receptivity to all the components of language, that is, going beyond the lexical meaning of the word and being sensitive to what it is made of, that is sound and rhythm. In this manner Dr. Grassi enriches the notion of analytic listening.

In this volume, we can appreciate the depth and quality of the contribution of Dr. Grassi as a musician, scholar and psychoanalyst. One will find in this book theoretical contributions as well as rich clinical examples from her experience with individuals and families. The nine chapters present different facets of Dr. Grassi's clinical and theoretical research. Some of these topics deal with music and temporality, music and primal relationships, intimacy and the negative in music, the musical unconscious in the family. The book ends with a chapter on the topic of sound and music during the COVID-19 pandemic.

Ludovica Grassi has brilliantly put together this new volume that enriches the Psychoanalytic Ideas and Application Series. The result is an important contribution which will surely be of interest to the psychoanalytic community and to all people interested not only in music and psychoanalysis but also in the way a deep understanding of music enriches the theory and practice of psychoanalysis.

Foreword

Early in her adult life, Ludovica Grassi considered becoming a concert pianist. It is a gift to psychoanalysis and the understanding of unconscious psychic life that she became instead a child and adult psychoanalyst. I first met her at the IPA Congress in Buenos Aires in 2017 where I chaired a paper session in which she presented. Her paper was an inspiring introduction to the deep relationship between music and psychoanalysis. As a returning student of music throughout the epochs of my life, I have always enjoyed a nourishing sense of emotional connection when I spend time at the piano. The origins and evolution of such rich experience have become profoundly clear through reading *The Sound of the Unconscious: Psychoanalysis as Music*.

As a musician, scholar and psychoanalyst, Dr Grassi takes us on a transformative journey. She makes clear we all have music in our souls; it underlies how we listen and how we apprehend human experience. Through her intellectual discoveries and her fine clinical examples, she makes the fundamental role of music in the development and functioning of unconscious mental life and affective experience clear.

As a scholar, Grassi is a master at interdisciplinary discovery. We are introduced to scientific connections between psychoanalysis and ethnomusicology, acoustemology, evolutionary musicology, bio-anthropology and neuroscience. Foreign territories become lively and intriguing as she explores the interrelated texture and structure of music and psychic development from a variety of scientific viewpoints.

Acoustemology is the creation of Steven Feld (1990), the ethnomusicologist and anthropologist, who introduced Grassi to a primitive society in Papua New Guinea where the Bosavi live. In their society, 'songs are vocalized mappings of the rainforest and sung from a bird's perspective; birds are considered to be what humans become after death: "gone reflections" or absence turned into presence, mainly through the sound of their voices' (see the Introduction). In this way we, too, are prepared for a journey that encompasses both earliest human development and mourning, the basic psychoanalytic themes of the book.

Grassi's contributions as a musician remind me of the Bosavis' experience of birds. She sees in music the mapping of the emerging unconscious mind; at the same time, she sees the presence of mourning, the delinking that opposes linking. Her understanding of music captures the merging of inner and outer, of living and lost. We learn that repetition, interval, silence and tempo express the subjectivity of the composer.

A notable moment in her book occurs when she introduces us to Bach as both creative transcriber, for example of Vivaldi concertos, and author of uncanny beauty in such works as the Goldberg Variations. She inspires us to wonder: how is it that the closing aria, which bookends thirty intervening *Variations* and has exactly the same notes as the opening aria, transforms into a touching farewell? As a psychoanalyst, I have been acutely aware that repetition of my patients' narratives and repetition of my interpretations occur. They vary but hold somehow true to basic themes. As a student of the piano, I know that my repetition of Debussy's Deux Arabesques No. 1 is never the same, though the notes are the same. The piece and I mature and change each time I relearn it, just as my patients and I mature in our repetitions of narrative and interpretation of meaning. While our shared understandings of conflict, trauma, neurotic and psychotic thinking evolve and mature, the notes of our first encounter are 'gone reflections' in our last encounter. The repetitions in between have turned the same notes into something familiar though different and our parting experience is both joyful and sad.

In psychoanalytic work repetition of narrative becomes meaningful through the very elements that structure music: rhythm, harmony, tone, timbre and silence. Musical structure is the foundation of unconscious psychic life. The earliest sounds of uterine life introduce levels of externality that both merge with and differentiate from the internal. The sounds are not just the crooning of the mother, or her traumatic outcries in less than optimal circumstances. They are the sounds of breath, blood flow, body fluid movement and there is silence. This is the ebb and flow, the somato-psychic foundation, of human experience.

Dr Grassi began, I believe, with an intuition that was deepened and confirmed in her psychoanalytic work with children, adults, couples and families. We read in her clinical examples, which include each of those constellations, how she recognizes and uses the music of individual and interrelated minds to understand and intervene. She anchors her insights in a brilliant integration of psychoanalytic theory as it has developed in relation to music from Freud to Laplanche to Ogden. As we accompany her on her journey as a musician, clinician and scholar, we become far more attuned to the origins, structure and musical profundity of psychic life.

Harriet L. Wolfe, MD, President-Elect, International Psychoanalytical Association

Introduction

It was only a few years ago when, some thirty years after I chose to give up a career as a musician, I came upon a book by Steven Feld (1990), an American ethnomusicologist and anthropologist, who introduced the discipline of *acoustemology*: he referred to the auditory and musical quality of human experience in different environments, from the urban context up to the rainforest milieu of Papua New Guinea, which was one of his favoured fields of research. The neologism conjoins the terms acoustics and epistemology, thereby theorizing 'sound as a way of knowing with and through the audible, an experiential nexus of sonic sensation' (Feld, 2017, pp. 84, 85): a relational view of knowledge through sound production and listening and their mutual relatedness, where subject–subject relationships replace subject–object ones. According to Feld: 'Life is shared with others-in-relation, with numerous sources of action that are variously human, non-human, living, non-living, organic, or technological' (ibid., p. 87). In Bosavi society, songs are vocalized mappings of the rainforest and sung from a bird's perspective; birds are considered to be what humans become after death: 'gone reflections' or absence turned into presence, mainly through the sound of their voices. In this exchange of different beings, the significance ascribed to transitional representations, such as the passage from life to death, is remarkable.

As a result of discovering the impressive field of acoustemology, new and different paths opened up in front of me. Inspired by Feld's work, I began a journey through literature to meet the many scholars and thinkers who, from different points of view, tried to overturn the priority that visual perception had been given over the other senses as the main or unique instrument of knowledge since Plato and Aristotle. Of course, I was fully aware that listening is the main tool of psychoanalysis, which has been focused, since its beginning, on verbal language. As a consequence, psychic activity has been formulated as centred on preconscious and conscious word representations, with an acoustic root, and, above all, on unconscious thing-presentations, chiefly consisting in visual images. Furthermore, the pervasive presence of sound, rhythm and music in human experience induced me to think about their importance from prenatal life onwards, and to reflect on the possible role of music in the development and functioning of psychic life and, more specifically, of the unconscious psyche.

Perhaps the scarce interest of psychoanalysts for the musical features of psychic life originated in Freud's alleged deafness to music, which has often been referred to as inexplicable, when compared with his creation of the *talking cure*, grounded in a human relationship and dialogue, with the *word* as its main tool. Moreover, although the main discovery of psychoanalysis was the unconscious, musical a-semantic language seemed to be much too close to the undifferentiated and the unknown, the realm of that oceanic feeling that Freud denied having ever experienced. The first generation of psychoanalysts produced a few studies on musical phenomena, pieces of music and the relationships between musicians' biographies and their creations. Among Wednesday Psychological Society attendants, Max Graf (1947), Little Hans's father, who was a musicologist and music critic, wrote an essay about the psychology of the musical composition process. However, the obscure and traumatic quality of music was still emphasized by Kohut and Levarie (1950), who suggested the implication of a conscious and unconscious working of Ego defences and organizing mechanisms in order to integrate and give meaning to the musical experience, felt as incomprehensible and, as such, traumatizing.

Theodor Reik redirected psychoanalysts' attention to the auditory dimension, somewhat neglected by a psychoanalysis centred on visual images in representation processes: sound and musical forms are closer to unconscious as well as affective movements. *Listening with the third ear* (Reik, 1948), to repeat the words in the title of Reik's book, facilitates unconscious communication between analyst and patient, and also fosters insight and surprise.

A number of psychoanalysts, from different parts of the world, have contributed since then to the advance of research on many music-related topics: similarities between musical and analytical listening and interpretation; relationships between forms of psychic suffering and musical expressions; analysis of musical languages and compositional styles linked to biographical studies of musicians; investigations on verbal contents of pieces of music, such as operas, vocal music, and musicians' suggestions; titles and related descriptive or anecdotical elements; theories of musicotherapy; the use of musical concepts in order to describe psychic elements or processes; the role of music as the best language to express emotions; the examination of isomorphisms between music and psychic activity.

A few colleagues began to study and work with the primal rhythmic and sound experiences in the mother–infant relationship. Suzanne

Maiello (1995, 2011) identified the *sound object* as the sum of auditory and rhythmic memories originated in foetal life: presence and absence are experienced by the foetus through the sound of its mother's voice, resulting in the constitution of a prenatal proto-object and, possibly, in the earliest mother–infant bond. Björn Salomonsson (2007), who founded infant psychoanalysis together with Johan Norman (2001, 2004), emphasizes the role of containment and, more specifically, the *music of containment* implied in such therapeutic relationships (Salomonsson, 2011). His work is based on the realization that babies can engage in dialogues with their analysts, as far as they understand the emotive, unconscious meaning of their analysts' messages and can convey their own emotional states through behaviour and/or sound utterances.

My passionate exploration led me to discover a rich trove of available research, carried out by eminent neuroscientists, developmental psychologists, psycholinguists and psychobiologists, about relationships between music, the mind and human communication. But what struck me most was the discovery of the new field of biomusicology, a term coined by the Swedish Nils Wallin in 1991 to comprehend evolutionary musicology, neuromusicology and comparative musicology. From then on, the book he published in 2000 with Björn Merker and Steven Brown became a faithful and revelatory companion on my own journey through the intertwinings of music and psychoanalysis and towards the origins of psychic life.

I came to realize that, although differences are often emphasized between language and music, the structure of music works in a very similar way in respect to the psyche's way of functioning. On the one hand, in Susanne Langer's writings (1942, 1951) I met the idea that musical structure is isomorphic to the movement of inner psychic life because of its sequences of motion and rest, its varying moments of expansion and withdrawal, the alternation of consonance and dissonance, of expectation and satisfaction, with climaxes of excitation and sudden falls into icy immobility; and all this without the oppositions of signifier/signified, or form/content. According to Langer (1942), music is a *significant form* or *unconsummated symbol*, able to express something virtual that unfolds only in time and is born from silence. Furthermore, I found out that, despite the well-established belief in the superior efficacy and precision of verbal language compared to the vagueness of music, a common precursor has been theorized for both, giving them equal status. Other evidence even seems to prove that language developed out of music: the hominization process appears to have evolved in close connection with the origins of music.

Music and language have more features in common than might be expected at first sight, such as melody, rhythm, grammar, syntax, tone and much else besides, similarities that are best appreciated in poetry. Indeed, the original intersection of music and language lies in poetry, since in ancient times music was exclusively vocal and poetry was always sung. The word, which is our main working resource, consists more of sound, rhythm and intonation than of lexical meaning, and it is precisely these components and their sensory traces of the earliest experiences, impossible to translate into conscious representations, that open up to the unconscious phantasy and the need to be focused on by analytic listening. The voice is the embodied aspect of sound production and perception: one's own voice, as well as the other's, touches through its vibrations the innermost areas of the psyche-soma, building and enriching the tactile and sound envelope that is the Ego-skin. According to Feld, voice is to the body what water is to land. 'The voice connects the many parts of the body; by resounding in the head and chest, the full body is always present in the "flow" of the voice, just as the connections of land are always present in the "flow" of water' (Feld, 1994, p. 12). Timbre, which allows identification of an individual's voice (as well as a musician's style), is a musical component involved in family psychic transmission and in positioning the newborn into the generational chain.

At the beginning, I was particularly impressed by the central role of time and rhythm both in music and in psychic life. Rhythm, as everybody knows, is one of the three main components of music, the others being melody and harmony. Music, defined as *the art of sounds in the movement of time*, is not only made up of development but also of imitation and repetition, in their creative dimension, and is involved in the repeated translations by the psyche of primal perception signs and memory-traces. Moreover, the work of mourning and the work of the negative are part and parcel of its structure. Music unfolds through linking and unlinking – the modus operandi of drives – through replacements and silences, regressions and anticipations.

According to psychoanalysis, human temporality is very different from physical time: the former is affected by unconscious timelessness and ruled by a discontinuous way of functioning that is based on two separate times and moves in opposite directions (afterwardsness or *après-coup*). Time is also a pivotal component of both the analytic setting, in its dual articulation of continuity and discontinuity, and the psychic work in the analytic process, where both progression and regression, anticipation and delay, closeness and rupture characterize unconscious transformations and the transference relationship.

The evolutive function of rhythm is to be found not only in the easy flow of mother–infant mutual exchanges but also in its inherent element of rupture, which opens up a space of absence and the inherent expectation, thereby originating representation. Temporal and rhythmic nuclei, binary structured, could be, in my view, the primordial frame of reference that enables the dawning psyche to signify stimuli that were meaningless up to that point; a process that can be traced in prenatal life, when auditory ability develops long before visual sensitivity. Rhythm and, more generally, temporality, rooted in the somato-psychic being, are key features of subjectivity and symbolic functions, as well as of music, as this involves identical physical vibratory phenomena.

The work of mourning, embedded in time, is the essence of both psychic life and musical structure, in which memory, too, has a basic function of linkage and signification. Music unfolds through an uninterrupted creation and disruption of sounds, leading to the final silence and void, but also to a deep inner transformation of the listener.

Silence is the condition for music to occur, a potential space in which a generative process may spring or a sound void for the infant to negatively hallucinate her/his mother and initiate representational activity. Accordingly, psychoanalysis requires a negative, de-signifying listening to enable the psychoanalyst to contact the patient's and the analyst's own sexual infantile: absence is the intersubjective basis of psychic life, the uncanny otherness that allows two subjects to communicate. Similarly, in music the intervals, or what is found in between sounds, confer musical meaning to a sequence of sounds. Even noise can help us approach our patients' psychic life and sufferings. Psychoanalytic listening has the same features as musical listening: passive, not adjustable but also active, through a ceaseless work of linking and unlinking, signification and de-signification. It is a process of creative construction that originates in the encounter between listener and object, both musical and psychoanalytic, from outside and inside ourselves.

Acknowledging the isomorphism between the working of both music and the psyche widens the range of both perceivable clinical elements and feasible interventions that are available to psychoanalysts. Considering music as a primal and inherent characteristic of psychic structure allows radical progresses to be achieved in our understanding of psychic working and origins, opening our minds to fruitful and high-value hypotheses. With our patients we can experience the use of different temporalities by analyst and patient, ruptures and recoveries of temporality in the analytic process, or the building up of temporality by children who were not allowed to develop their own sense of time. The analyst's and patients' musical and sensory features of body, word and voice convey the largest extent of contents and movements from their own psychic life. We cannot do without music in order to approach the earliest psychic motions, as well as the most primitive experiences and functioning. Even in prenatal life, when the primal sensory organization happens to be torn before the mother–infant bond can be established, rhythmical and sound components of primary processes are undermined, but can be resumed and worked out later in the analytic relationship. What is needed, I would emphasize, is to go beyond the application of psychoanalysis to music in order to achieve a musically informed psychoanalysis.

In this book, I would like to illustrate a path of clinical and theoretical research, based on the evidence that music is a basic organizational principle for the psyche, since it uses similar processes and mechanisms, and plays a pivotal role in the development of psychic functions, such as symbolization and relatedness. The unconscious, the keystone of psychoanalysis, appears to be endowed with a musical nature. The awareness of musical components of psychic functioning enhances both our receptivity to all the components of language and our sensibility to the specific level at which the patient is functioning. The theoretical framework I am proposing intends to facilitate working with different and simultaneous functioning levels of patients, as well as developing specific research areas that are involved with primal sensory experiences, subjectivation and the origins of symbolic functions.

Chapter 1

Sound and rhythm in psychic life and psychoanalytic work*

> We do not know of any human society that lacks music, we do not know of a single society that does not express itself through dance.
> Simha Arom (2000)

Music and its history make up a whole with human civilization and the process of hominization since the origins of mankind. In ancient Greek culture, music always came along and was intertwined with the development of poetry, which it probably preceded. Homer was represented as a blind bard who accompanied himself on the cithara: blindness referred to his being intent on his internal world from where his verses drew on the deepest and innermost motions. Greek *mousiké* encompassed melody, dance and poetry, whose common denominator is rhythm. Greeks held music in high regard, as is testified by the countless myths that attribute it with immense powers, mainly over the spirit and the will: Orpheus fascinated and bewitched wild animals, plants and even rocks with his singing; Amphion built the walls of Thebes with the sound of music; Arion was saved from death by dolphins, enchanted by his singing (Mila, 1963).

The supremacy of sight

And yet both humanistic and scientific knowledge has been constructed around the visual element as the prevalent or exclusive instrument of knowledge (from scientific observation to philosophical or metaphysical representation), depriving the acoustic element of commensurate appreciation. In the history of knowledge, Plato first and then Aristotle (*De*

---

* A version of this chapter was previously published as 'The dimension of sound and rhythm in psychic structuring and analytic work' in *The Italian Psychoanalytic Annual*, (2014) 1914: 63–82.

anima or *On the Soul*) had arranged the instruments of perception according to a hierarchical and evaluative system that was to influence philosophical reflection for centuries to come: classical culture thus developed as a culture of the icon, which confers on the image the value of ontological proof through which knowledge (de-*monstration*) is possible. Not only epistemologically but also at the level of brain functioning, sight and hearing influence each other, with a tendency of the first to prevail over the second: according to some psychological research, when sight and hearing conflict, our brain chooses sight.

Despite these epistemological and ontological biases having led to a relative atrophying of the aural/oral dimension, in favour of a strong link of the 'scopic' regime to the subject's cognitive and rational sphere (Midolo, 2008), sound, an intrusive and pervasive phenomenon, is an indispensable communicative medium and relational resource within an individual's experience and social life. Along these lines, G. Simmel, M. Weber and T. W. Adorno introduced a perspective according to which music is the interpretive key and articulatory means of social and identification processes in every specific cultural reality.

According to Jacques Attali (1977, p. 3): 'For twenty-five centuries, Western knowledge has tried to look upon the world. It has failed to understand that the world is not for the beholding. It is for hearing. It is not legible, but audible.' Writing, too, may be considered as an affirmation of the visual over the oral, leading to the view that the oral tradition is an archaic remnant.[1] Sight operates along straight lines, therefore according to a linear (two-dimensional) and sequential mode, which favours the logics of exclusion: in fact, the rational mind, abstract thought and detached logic that lead to looking at reality through objective eyes are associated with it. Hearing, on the contrary, is multidirectional and three-dimensional, and also more rooted in corporeality (through its association with vibrations), in physicalness, and, likewise, in the inner world: if the gaze is directed to observing the external dimension that is foreign to the subject, hearing is the organ of reflection, of introjection, of the possibility for listening to one's own *daimon*, as well as having great evocative and generative power per se.

With its multiple declinations (voices, noises, rhythms and harmonies), sound saturates the subject's daily experience: hearing is both a sensorial experience open to indiscriminate and painfully passive reception and an indispensable medium for producing meaning. Jacques Lacan, too, emphasized the phonetic value of the *signifier*, in that it is an acoustic image that transmits the concept.

Only recently, a new science has emerged to bridge this gap, *acoustemology* (Feld, 1990, 2003), which, defining itself through a word derived from 'acoustics' and 'epistemology', aims to analyse reality by using sound and listening, as well as their reflective feedback, as the preferred mode for knowing about and living in the world. Starting from the idea of an anthropology of sound meant to decolonize ethnomusicology's disciplinary paradigms, Feld came up with a definition of acoustemology as the science that uses the different sound ways of being in the world and of knowing it: these range beyond music and the spoken word to include unconventional tools of knowledge that come from an ensemble of broader sound environments, of which music is one of many expressions. For example, studying the soundscapes of the populations of the rainforests of New Guinea, which live in close contact with birds and their song, or those of the city populations of the Western world, Feld constructed a sort of acoustic ecology and anthropology that allows a significant in-depth analysis of our knowledge about worlds that are so very different. Acoustemology basically relies on a relational understanding of the human and non-human world, that is, an existential relationality. Participation and reflection make acoustemology a kind of processual and experiential, subject–subject knowledge.

The origins of music

The new field of evolutionary musicology has shed light on the inextricable interweaving between the evolution of music and the evolution of man's social structures, group functions and cultural expressions. Various evolutionary theories have attempted to explain how selective pressures determined the origins of man's capacity to produce and enjoy music: as an instrument for courting and selecting one's sexual companion; as a function capable of furthering coordination, cohesion and cooperation in the social group; as a means for improving parent–child communication with a resulting increase in the survival of newborns. In this way music flanks language in the study of man's evolution from his animal forefathers.

One of the most promising aspects of this research focuses on the interface between music and language and on the evolutionary roots of this relationship: intonational phonology, which analyses the melodic element of language,[2] and metrical phonology, which centres on the rhythmic forms of discourse,[3] are two examples of this link, alongside the studies on the relationship between verbal language and gesture, which we may compare to the relationship between music and dance. According to the semiologist Jean Molino (2000), music and language share numerous elements, among which melody, rhythm, affective semantics and also syntax. A clear example of something that was originally both music and language is poetry, which was always sung, while music at the beginning was exclusively vocal. Rhythm and imitation would give rise to that step in the evolutionary passage[4] towards the capacity of representation, which is *mimetic culture*: activities of collective imitation accompanied by vocalizations and organized by rhythm would develop into the first forms of narrative, from which rites and myths subsequently emerged.

According to the Swedish neuroscientist Steven Brown (2000), music and language testify to the evolution of an identical precursor, which he calls *musilanguage*. This was an emotional–referential communicative system that used vocal sounds in their dual quality of emotional and referential meaning. The specific characteristics subsequently developed by music would make it the chosen instrument for furthering identity, coordination, cohesion and the sharing of emotions on a group level. In fact, differently from language, which necessarily proceeds by alternation, music fosters concurrence, and consequently interpersonal harmonization, through its vertical dimension, built up by harmony (the simultaneous production of different sounds) and by rhythm. This is why mechanisms of individual selection alone would not be enough to explain its origins, in which processes of group selection, or of cultural groups, perhaps played their part.

Rhythm, the temporal core of music, is shared by man and animals insofar as it is about the capacity to move rhythmically, whereas the skill that enables movements to be synchronized to an external rhythm is specifically human (with rare and limited exceptions) and distinct from the capacity to produce and perceive the tonal elements of music. This ability, which comes under the generalized phenomenon in nature of *entrainment*, depends on the experience of a regular rhythm that allows us to predict the next beat so that we can synchronize our behaviour to the external pulse. Its selective advantage, by coordinating sound production, has been hypothesized in the possibility that the intensity and therefore the sound diffusion produced by calls having varying objectives (sexual, feeding, danger and so on) would be greatly increased. From this point of view, the acquisition of musical and dancing skills could constitute in man an indispensable precursor to the birth of a referential language (Merker, 2000).

However, other interpretations in an evolutionary key of the development of man's musical skills are possible, starting from the condition of *neoteny* (or *altriciality*, as scholars of evolution call it) where the young human is born quite helpless and totally dependent on the adult. At this level, music would play a crucial role in activating specific affiliative mechanisms, not only through maternal vocalizations but also through the whole range of temporally structured rhythmic communicative interactions (movements, glances, facial expressions, vocalizations, contact...), which coordinate the emotions of the dyad and encourage the relationship. Given the capacity of the newborn to trans-modally process sensory information,[5] the channel of communication (acoustic, visual, tactile, kinaesthetic) used by the mother and child would be less important than its temporal structure, the rhythm. Not because mother and infant must necessarily synchronize their rhythms, but so that they can follow the variations introduced by the other and may both satisfy the anticipation and open themselves up to something new (Dissanayake, 2000).

Research in the neurophysiological field has shown the fundamental role that music plays not only in cognitive development but also, and above all, in the relational capacities of human beings. Walter Freeman (2000), a Californian neurobiologist, has come to the conclusion that trust, the basic foundation for every one of man's social activities, originates from the experience of music and from the deep interpersonal bonds that it alone can create. Neurophysiological research has shown that knowledge is the result of autonomous neuronal activities that replace the schemes of activity produced by external stimuli. Thus, there is no direct transfer of knowledge from the outside, but a highly individual internal process of constructing knowledge, starting from the meaning that the external stimuli hold for each single individual. This results in what Freeman calls *epistemological solipsism*. Starting out from this unequivocal fact, how can the mind enter into communication with another to organize coherent and efficient collective behaviour, and how can a relationship of trust be established between minds that makes the appearance and use of language possible?

Freeman postulates that music is first of all a biological construction technique of the social bond, which would operate by means of neuro-humoral mechanisms similar to those activated in the parental bond and which, by determining the dissolution of previous learning and the loosening of the relative neuronal synaptic links, open up opportunities for new acquisitions and behaviours based on understanding and sharing. By involving the whole body through the somato-sensory and motor systems of both the person producing it and the person participating in it through listening, dancing or other rhythmical movements, music lays the basis for coordination, cooperation and communication within groups. Opening up to what is new and at the same time to what is expected, music allows a sense of trust and reliability to develop that makes communication, sharing and life possible[6] (similarly to the Winnicottian concepts of 'going on being' and 'transitionality').

Music and psychoanalysis

At the beginning, psychoanalysis paid little attention to music – the art of time par excellence – perhaps because it was difficult to articulate with an unconscious whose basic quality is timelessness;[7] and yet the *talking* cure originated as a treatment method based on the word, which is a specific type of sound production. Freud (1914) justified his own incapacity to appreciate music as having little physiological predisposition for it and, above all, because of the difficulty in using a rational or analytic approach to it. Barale and Minazzi (2008) and Barale (2008) compare Freud's drawing back from the unknown and the undifferentiated in the a-semantical language of music to Breuer's recoiling from the irruption of the transference. In a letter to Fliess (31 August 1898, in Masson, 1985), written while he was working on *The Interpretation of Dreams*, Freud expressed his admiration for the work by Theodor Lipps *Grundtatsachen des Seelenlebens* (The Basic Facts of Psychic Life; 1885–1905), in which he found many connections with the discoveries he was making at that moment. However, he said he had stopped reading at the chapter 'The Relationships Between Sounds', justifying himself with 'the atrophy of my acoustic sensibilities' (Masson, 1985, p. 325). According to Barale and Minazzi, Freud stopped because the questions posed by Lipps 'would have shifted the focus of research on the "basic facts of psychic life" from the representational unconscious (and from the vicissitudes of infantile sexuality) to a substantially pre-representational dimension, which was excessively "dissonant" with Freud's expectations and requirements at this time' (Barale and Minazzi, 2008, p. 945). The founding act of psychoanalysis required the field to be defined: focused on the representational unconscious and on infantile sexuality, it had to exclude the language of music since it was a-semantic and so not suitable for psychoanalytic interpretation. In his turn, Lipps had explored in depth the bases of individual empathy, identifying them in *internal imitation*, a concept recently revived by neuroscientists with the term *intentional consonance*, a phenomenon closely interwoven with rhythm and with what has been called *embodied simulation* (Gallese, 2007; 2009a, b).

More recently, increasing interest in the non-verbal and early aspects of interpersonal relationships has meant that music has made its appearance as the object of psychoanalytic reflection. However, the arduous task of getting into the specific language of musical expression remains, which often leads to merely focusing attention on musicians' biographies or on the analysis of characters or plots in opera librettos, or else to restrictively using musical metaphors or analogies to describe aspects of the psychoanalytic situation (from Edoardo Weiss's *resonance identification*, to Bion's *being in unison*, up to Salomonsson's *playing chamber music in the analyst's consulting room*, to give just a few examples). Something that Freud (1904) had in fact already done, in quoting the words of Hamlet to the courtier Guildenstern:

> You would play upon me, you would seem to know my stops, you would pluck out the heart of my mystery, you would sound me from my lowest note to the top of my compass; and there is much music, excellent voice in this little organ, yet cannot you make it speak. 'Sblood, do you think I am easier to be played on than a pipe? Call me what instrument you will, though you can fret me, you cannot play upon me.
>
> (Shakespeare, *Hamlet*, Act 3, scene 2, lines 352–360)

Here what is highlighted of the shared aspect between music and psychoanalysis is the need for a player and the fact that this player can do nothing but interpret, so that every musical or psychoanalytical realization is the result and product of at least two people. Similarly, Freud compares the analyst to a skilful musician who plays upon the psyche of the patient in such a way as to create a harmonious composition (letter to Fliess of 2 November 1901: Freud, 1887–1902, p. 486).

Music bases its poietic power on interpretation, which is also the main tool of psychoanalysis: both interpretations (musical and psychoanalytical) enable light to be shed on what at first sight is not written on the score (of the musician) or in the narration (of the patient). The player and the analyst read/listen to the secondary language that the composer/analysand has left on the score/narration, grasping the primary language that expresses its deepest affective meaning (Mancia, 1998).

The most fascinating aspect of music, which promises interesting openings also for psychoanalysis, is its dual rootedness in reason and affects; it is governed by physical and mathematical laws, but at the same time is able to express and delve into the most secluded refuges of human emotions. For Susanne Langer (1951), the language of music is isomorphic to the movement of psychic life, rather than to specific mental contents. Music allows emotions to be intensely experienced without in any way defining their object or content. Form and content lose their differentiation in music and tend to coincide: it is a symbolic creation but does not present anything but itself, with no reference to an object that is different from itself. On the contrary, rather than referring to latent contents, it seems to give expression to the virtual, to something that must unfold in the temporal space in which it begins and ends, leaving silence behind it. *Pure form*, an empty signifier according to the musicologist Hanslick (1854), *significant form* and *unconsummated symbol*, for Langer (1942), are all definitions that refer to the annulling of the opposition signifier/signified. These concepts closely approach Anzieu's *formal signifier* (1987), which defines a preliminary form of psychic structure, a 'precognitive factor, on the mind–body boundary, thanks to which an internal space that is suitable for the symbolizing processes can be traced out. The formal signifier gives meaning to preverbal communication, without restricting it precociously to precise meanings ... it lacks definite meaning but is rich in "sense"' (Di Benedetto, 2000, p. 186).

Di Benedetto integrates the concepts of Langer and Anzieu, speaking of open symbolic forms or unsaturated symbols, and comes to the conclusion that:

> Music, the bearer of 'significant forms', helps to construct internally 'formal signifiers', in other words, it sensitizes the perception of events on the border between the psychic and the somatic. Offering

psychoanalysis a pertinent structure for the sensory sphere, of a pre-symbolic nature, it makes the more obscure and dreaming part of the psyche more alive and enables the conscious to fore-hear it.

(Di Benedetto, 2000, p. 186)

Consequently, the musical experience could sensitize both the analyst's listening skills, allowing 'precognition of the unconscious via somatic paths', and the capacity for offering, through the infra-verbal aspects of the interpretation, an expressive configuration of the patient's unconscious contents that are far from the representative level. The musical element, an early primal quality of language (see Steven Brown's *musilanguage* model, 2000), fusing together action, emotion and proto-thought into an undifferentiated whole, enables one to go beyond understanding of the communicated contents and thus open up to participation and a shared experience.

Art bound up with the passing of time creates and destroys because every new sound destroys the preceding one:

> As long as it lasts, music provides, with a copious offering of sound, the equivalent of a comforting presence, and then plunges those who abandon themselves to it into mourning, since it leaves behind an absence that no plastic art produces. It is a form that transports and illudes, creating an envelope of beautiful sensations, destined, though, to dissolve shortly afterwards in a silence that disilludes and wounds. A form capable of rousing an impression of fullness, followed by emptiness.
>
> (Di Benedetto, 2000, p. 168)

Mancia (1998), taking his cue from a passage in Freud's essay *On Transience*, points out the inner temporal essence of music, which differentiates it from other spatial aesthetic objects in that it is a code of signification that flows through time and is enjoyed over time: the diachrony of music is therefore opposed to the synchrony of spatial arts.

In music's unfolding (both when listening and when playing), there is a continuous articulation between the expectation and the mnestic recovery, a continuous separating of completed forms before the discovery of new ones: a constant proposing, therefore, of an uninterrupted series of mournings, like enigmatic and unavoidable moments in the face of continuous transformations that the musical forms undergo, along the linear path of time.

Only the work of memory can give meaning and continuity to the succession of sounds and silences, making them relate to each other, but also subjectifying them and linking the present affective experience to old emotions that have given shape to the inner world.

Time and rhythm in psychoanalysis

Time, one of the primary elements of music, plays a pivotal and particularly complex role in psychoanalytic theorizing, as Green (2001) has reminded us when describing in Freud's thinking a *tree of time* in which different and apparently incompatible temporalities are associated and superimposed, which certainly cannot be referred back to any genetic linear logic. Starting from the timelessness that characterizes the unconscious and from the repeated digression from ordinary time that takes place in dreams, to the diphasic but also discontinuous temporality (fixations, infantile amnesia) of the libidinal development and to the mnestic gaps produced by repression, the timeline is reversed in the regression of the neurosis to infantile fixations and in the forwards-backwards-moving process of the *après-coup*, broadening to encompass the phylogenetic origins of the primal phantasies and the function of the superego as a bond between generations. The alternative forms assumed by non-recoverable memories (the compulsions to repeat, hallucinatory states, actings) and the denial of time in situations dominated by the destructive drives, leading to a shattered time, are added to all of this (Green, 2000, 2002).

Time constitutes one of the components of the space–time unit established by the setting[8] that, while being antithetical towards a-temporality and to the absence of organization of the unconscious, provides containment for the patient's free associations and for the analyst's freely fluctuating attention, thus allowing the analytic relationship and the interpretative work to unfold. Time in all its declinations, and above all in the bipolar form of continuity/discontinuity, is the essential element of the psychoanalytic process, which Petrella (2004) has represented through the intense metaphor of 'Gradiva', the *advancer*. The time element is fundamental in the model of a transformation made possible by activation of the alpha function and involvement of the passing through of mourning, and is further complicated by the fact that the psychoanalytic process is carried out in the two-person sphere of the relationship, thus interlapping with the temporalization of the participating subjects.

Melissa has a life rhythm based on three working days a week in another town while the others are lived with her companion. She came to ask for my help with her current difficulty of making a decision about her future place of stay, as well as a series of other issues that are particularly important for her. In fact, she has many projects, and while she is going through them I ask myself how she has enough time to do so many things: work, university, sport, family … Every now and then she pauses and asks me: 'Am I going too fast?', referring to the way she talks and to the uninterrupted succession of themes introduced, among which also her desire to have a child, which she shares with her companion; but for the moment, she can't manage to get into an *expectant* frame of mind, as though it is too soon for her, but at the same time too late. She tells me that she always has a headache on the days she spends in the city she works in, and the next time she begins by saying that she always has a headache when she comes here. She seems to be always hurrying towards a destination that is somewhere else; she gives me the impression of an upbeat rhythm[9] that never finds a supporting downbeat or moment of rest. It emerges that she is the daughter of very young parents who 'did not realize they were parents': as a child, she used to flee the chaos at home for the calm of her grandparents' house. I have the feeling that she is actually asking me to help her find her own rhythm that she can feel comfortable with, which she has never been able to develop from the rhythm she shared during the earliest phases of her life. But will she be able to wait the time necessary to carry through an analytic process?

In a slightly later stage of our therapeutic work we more specifically tackle the effort needed to adapt to rhythms that never seem to be her own. An intervention of mine about how she feels as a newborn breastfed at fixed times rather than on demand led to the emerging of a memory, or rather of a story told by her mother, who, moreover, has always refused to talk about her pregnancy and Melissa's early childhood. When, as a baby, Melissa woke up at night demanding milk, her mother used to prepare a cup of milk and some biscuits for herself at the same time; she enjoyed this ritual to such an extent that when Melissa no longer required these nightly feeds she began to wake the baby up on purpose so that she didn't miss out on what had become a pleasurable habit. Time is a central element in our therapeutic relationship, which Melissa initially perceived as rigid and inflexible, later enjoying the opportunity for asking, and obtaining, to move an appointment on an occasion that did not depend on her not being able to come.

However, our therapeutic work could not really begin until Melissa, in the session before the Christmas holidays, tells me that she has decided to stop the analysis. This sort of therapy does not suit her; she needs help that focuses more on her uncertainties and hesitancies; moreover, my silences leave her feeling abandoned and lost in the fragmentary state of her mental life. She makes me feel like a little-present parent who, absorbed in her own narcissistic issues, does not know how to give her child nutritious and easily digestible food and, most of all, who asks her child yet again to adapt to rhythms that are foreign to her. Above all, I feel Melissa's anguish at being sucked back down into the emptiness and solitude of her origins, if the other does not make her literally 'feel/hear' her/his presence. My attention to her difficulties and, above all, my recognition of her profound need for a structuring sound containment, whereby we can create a rhythm that is not only mine but not even totally hers either, allowed her to come back after the holidays convinced of being able to find something good in our sessions, while I, too, felt less constricted by the forced feeding that the quick rhythm of her discourse had imposed on me.

The setting is also structured by the rhythmic component that characterizes it, both the regular repetition over time of the meetings between analyst and patient, and its beginnings and endings (of discourse, of the sessions, of the week, of the periods of work alternating with holidays, of the conclusion). The session takes shape by placing itself in an ongoing process not only within the analytic path but also in the limited space of the session: it is very different if a silence, a certain content, or a rush of emotion occurs at the beginning, at the end, or during a specific moment of the development of the analyst–patient relationship.

Luisa's sessions follow a particular rhythm: they begin with a long silence that I initially feared was hostile, perhaps due to the idea of a comparison with the psychotherapists who had preceded me, followed by a pretty fluent piece of discourse, which I felt I interrupted just as I was concluding the session; Luisa, too, reacts with surprise and disappointment, leaving me with the impression that I have wronged her and that, in any case, our times do not coincide. Even more, perhaps, I am struck by the particular intonation of her voice – monotonous, the words tied together. This painful perception of silences and interruptions helps us to work on an episode from the first period of analysis when, having had to be absent for a week, she had asked to make up the sessions lost by fitting them into the weeks before and after her absence, saturating them with sessions. It also helps us to tackle later, after the summer, issues that revolve around emptiness and fullness, and in particular her difficulty in tolerating voids. Luisa bears a deep nucleus of suffering linked to the very early experience of her family's emigration and to the loss of her mother, who left her at a very young age with two siblings and an affectionate father who obviously had difficulty in combining an artistic career with family needs. Despite having cried in the first session when speaking of her mother's death, which, besides, occurred in circumstances that aroused in me the fantasy that she could have committed suicide, Luisa did not seem to me to be ready to face this subject, which I imagine (perhaps wrongly) to have been extensively dealt with in her preceding therapies.

She describes how in her relationships she behaves as though the other is excessively powerful compared to her, and as though she has to do the impossible ('hang herself') to make and maintain contact. Until the moment when in one session she speaks of how little it would take to help children who have been deprived of their depressed mothers' gaze, and of how much she herself used to develop intense attachments to young female figures who came into her family alongside the father as babysitters or companions. In this moment, I realize that I have finally succeeded in understanding something about the strange way of her prosody, which had struck me so much: she links her words together by lengthening the last vowel, which has the effect of softening the rhythm and of flattening the tonal oscillations and which deprives her way of talking of pauses, breaths, gaps and melodic motions. This is why I find it so difficult to conclude the sessions because there is never a point of arrival or pause in her phrasing. This is not only her way of attaching herself to me but also of expressing her diffidence, making any intervention extremely difficult as it tends to become a forced irruption, a break in continuity.

Concerning the sensory deprivation of the situation in which the analytic work is carried out, in the majority of cases debate focuses on visual excitation, limited by the use of the couch that does not allow glances between the analyst and analysand to meet, and on tactile excitation, avoided by a relationship that excludes physical contact; at times mention is made of the olfactory sense, as Anzieu (1985) exemplifies when writing of an *olfactory envelope*. Hearing, which has the basic characteristic of not being voluntarily adjustable, is obviously the privileged channel for analytic communication, between the analysand's discourse and the analyst's interpretation; but there are also bodily sounds and noises made by the movements of the analytic pair that merge into the overall background sound of the context (air conditioning, traffic...); and finally there are unexpected noises from outside, which lacerate the membrane of the setting and break the rhythms of the analytic couple.

During a session with Antonella, in analysis for about two years, strong blows from a hammer or pickaxe were heard from a neighbouring flat that did not cease for the whole hour. Antonella is greatly disturbed by this, experiencing it as a violent irruption, whose irregular rhythm corresponds to that of her anxiety and arouses catastrophic expectation. I interpret that she feels my para-excitatory function as insufficient, since it leaves her at the mercy of violent and undecipherable perceptions; Antonella replies that with all this noise even the slight ticking of the carriage clock disturbs her, which she doesn't usually notice. She feels the urge to block her ears with her hands, just as she used to do when she was little, when she heard noises coming from her parents' room; but, in actual fact, it still happens, whenever she returns to her family home. The regular ticking of the clock seems, instead, to represent my attentive presence during the sessions and gives her the reassuring feeling of a safe place in which absolute psycho-physical continuity is a given: a silent transference onto the context that becomes painfully noticeable when the protective screen is lacerated. This sound invasion of the setting reproposes the presence of the other as a forced break-in that takes her off-guard, defenceless and fragile, obliterating her capacity to think and feel, as well as the state of always being on the alert that characterizes her presence in her family. And the trauma of an abuse emerges suffered at the hands of her father shortly after the menarche had appeared, which had already caught her by surprise due to its precociousness, breaking the rhythm of her development. But this situation, in which I, too, became the abusing parent, at least permits her to experience the rage replaced up to that moment by an indestructible (and equally acrobatic) idealization of her father.

Rhythm at the origins of psychic life

The Italian encyclopaedia Treccani traces the origin of the word 'rhythm' back to the Greek word rèo, to flow. It defines rhythm as 'the ordered succession over time of forms of movement, and the frequency with which various phases of the movement follow each other; this succession can be perceived by the ear (in an alternation of sounds and pauses, of sounds that are more intense or less intense or similar), or by the eye (as an alternation of moments of light and shade, of actions and pauses, of actions that are similar to each other or actions that differ and so on) or conceived in memory and thought.'

Some basic rhythms combine the visual element, the sound element and other perceptive channels, such as, for example, those generated by the movements of the stars and planets: consequently, the alternation of light and dark, with all its inherent variations in forms and colours, sounds, smells and so on that accompany the alternation of day and night, corresponds on a psycho-somatic level to the succession of waking and sleeping, with the resulting succession of opening up and closing in the face of perceptive stimuli, but also of variations in physiological activities (e.g. cerebral electrical activity, the production of hormones and neurotransmitters, variations in muscular tone and so on). Sleep, despite the (partial) closure of the perceptive channels, nevertheless opens up to symbolization through the activity of dreaming, paving the way to a fundamental dimension for the theory, the clinical work and the origins themselves of psychoanalysis.

Rhythm is a crucial element in games for small children (peek-a-boo, give-and-take, *fort-da*...): there is always an interruption that generates an expectation, a generative void of what will become a representation of the absent stimulus. The game of the wooden reel (Freud, 1920) may be considered a prototype of the central significance of rhythm in psychological organization. It includes repetition, which, while Freud held it to be the most radical and invincible aspect of the drive, in this case, as in music, is already a working-through and symbolizing. It also includes anticipation, which signals psychic work taking the place of the perceptive void. Language (*fort, da*) comes later, when everything has already been worked out, as it were.

We must not forget that these rhythmic stimuli were in the first place physical (also because sounds and noises originate as vibrations often perceivable by receptors spread throughout the body, before being processed by our acoustic apparatus), making up the sound envelope that wraps the child even before she/he is born, when she/he is immersed in an environment that manifests itself essentially through tactile and acoustic stimuli: among these the heartbeat, the origin of a hypothetic proto-symbolization and perhaps of music. Suzanne Maiello (1995, 2011) has defined a *sound object* as 'the total whole of prenatal recollections of a sound and rhythmical nature that the child keeps in her/his memory after birth', including the maternal voice (2011, p. 249, author's translation).

The elements of continuity that made up the foundations for the homeostasis of the foetus's organism are interrupted at birth: the rhythm of meals replaces the continuous flow of nutritive substances through the umbilical cord; so does the rhythm between sucking and swallowing and relative pauses; the provision of oxygen previously supplied by a circulatory system shared with the mother must now be obtained by an autonomous respiratory rhythm, through a critical phase that includes a more or less protracted moment of apnoea; the continuous and re-assuring sound of the mother's heartbeat gives way to the newborn's autonomous cardiac activity, with completely different tonal and rhythmic characteristics; and the sounds of the mother's body are replaced by infinite sounds and noises from the external world, no longer muffled by the maternal container.

The opportunity for the child's psyche to establish itself in her/his body or for the initial somato-psychic unit not to suffer shifts, splits or seductions depends on the presence of a caring environment that ensures the repetition of feeding, the reopening of arms, the periodical production of sounds and sensory stimulations (everything that Freud included in the alternation between states of excitation and calm). The continuity of being that cannot stand excessive pressures or interruptions is a rhythmical time. According to Fornari (1984), the essence of rhythm is to establish a dynamic temporal specularity and to recreate it over and over again.

In her therapy work with children, Anna Baruzzi (1985) discovered the importance of sharing rhythmical experiences with another person in helping to get out of mental psychotic or autistic states, through overcoming a mechanic or inanimate way of functioning and gaining access to affects and vital experiences. While it is true that needs have rhythms, rhythm is itself a need and it lies at the origins of life. Baruzzi writes:

> The crucial issue seems to lie in the interval that permits the mnestic trace to be deposited while remaining sufficiently active for encountering new stimuli. The interval must be such that allows a bond, a relationship, a connection between the two elements in play, a

rhythmic polarity of oppositions whose relationship is to be enquired into through desire.
(Baruzzi, 1985, p. 251, author's translation)

Rhythm, understood as the alternation between sound and silence, or between different sounds, in a repetition that is only partly foreseeable, may constitute the root of the psyche as an apparatus functioning through temporal processes. The opposite of continuous is not discontinuous, but the unexpected. If the birth of time is possible only by starting from permanence, from the certainty of a Winnicottian *going on being*, then the event – the opposition of presence–absence – is needed to construct it, and to differentiate (André, 2009). Rhythm contains breaks and continuity; the break becomes what heralds continuity, and is a micro-space of absence, the primal particle of emptiness that is then occupied by the expectation of repetition and therefore by its representation. It makes up a miniature, an embryo, of the process that leads from absence to symbolization.

So rhythmic continuity of the experience and experiences of harmonic accord seem to be indispensable to mental birth, although the experiences of discontinuity seem to be equally indispensable. Disharmonies and the unexpected seem to be essential for the small foreign automa closed in the rhythms of his body–machine to gain access to the human and living world.
(Baruzzi, 1985, p. 252, author's translation)

Temporal and rhythmical microstructures could constitute the primal and prototypical schemes that the primordial psyche resorts to in order to decipher the stimuli still lacking meaning that come from inside and outside the body. This does not seem to be far from Conrotto's proposal (2011) on the basis of which the dividing line that creates the difference in binary logics (presence/absence, from which all the other oppositions derive, such as good/bad, pleasure/displeasure and so on) would constitute the first effective signifier opening up the path to knowledge. But Maiello (2011) pre-dated these processes, attributing to the maternal voice, characterized by qualitative constancy and by discontinuity over time, the function of introducing the principle of *difference* already in prenatal life. I would add that music in all its forms, starting from the most elementary components, includes and 'is isomorphic with the successions of tension/relaxation and waiting/resolution that characterize the first preverbal and imitative exchanges between a child and the human environment' (Barale and Minazzi, 2008, p. 948).

Rhythm adds to chronological, cosmic time the opportunity for absorbing the chance factor, the event, allowing them to be metabolized and historicized – although inevitably, in including absence, emptiness or negation, it implies death that does not belong to infinite cosmological time. It alludes to finiteness but is not a closed, circular time: perhaps we can better describe it as a spiral time. If we consider the time of the unconscious as a time without limits, or better, as a non-time, in that the unconscious 'ignores time', we can postulate that rhythm belongs to preconscious time and that initially it was the other's preconscious that lent its own rhythm which, connecting up to a pre-existing trace of internal rhythm, triggered the vicissitudes of the subjectivation process. With Laplanche (1989) we may centre on a human temporality that, detached from cosmological time, but also distinct from the time of the living organism, cannot but refer to a subjectivity in an active temporalizing movement in which the human being shows himself to be capable of producing or creating his own time, although always with the help of the other.

In 'A Note upon the "Mystic Writing-Pad"' (1925a), Freud introduces rhythm (here we are still in the time of the living organism) as a founding element of the perception of time starting from the discontinuous way in which perception of the external world functions, hypothesizing that 'cathectic innervations are sent out and withdrawn in rapid periodic impulses from within into the completely pervious system Pcpt.-Cs. ... I further had a suspicion that this discontinuous method of functioning of the system Pcpt.-Cs lies at the bottom of the origin of the concept of time' (p. 231). This periodic functioning could be motivated by the need for the conscious not to saturate itself with contents, so as to be able to welcome new perceptions; consequently, it would use moments of closure to empty itself of representations. Furthermore, the organism would protect itself from the aggression of external perceptions by diluting their intensity over time. In this way, what appears as a moment of closure and inertia acquires the value of a phase of transformation (which implies time) and of transfer (topical) (Laplanche, 1989).

When we think that Freud attempted to explain the qualitative perception of the internal sensations of pleasure and displeasure through a reduction or increase in tension of a given period of time (e.g. in *Beyond the Pleasure Principle*, 1920), we may conclude that rhythm for him is the essential element in both internal and external perception. But already in his first psychoanalytic writings, the notion of *Nachträglichkeit* opened up a temporal gap between two events and their signifying. Rediscovered and translated by Lacan as *après-coup*, it introduces the subject to a discontinuous time, 'a time of blows' (Laplanche, 2006), where these 'transported' (*tragen*) blows are interrupted by latent instants, resulting in a syncopated rhythm that derives from the interweaving of two different rhythmic trends. For these voids of representation and of memory processing, may we also think of the *après-coup*, 'made of eclipses and active

Sound and rhythm in psychic life 23

moments' (Laplanche, 2006), as a form of rhythm? Which, however, in the repetitive element associated to the two-way traffic of the arrow of time cannot be considered either closed circular time, which inexorably refers back to the past, or linear time that proceeds from the past to the present to the future. Perhaps in this case, too, we have a spiral time: the primal scene – which constituted a silent (but inscribed) trace due to the failure of symbolization, and was therefore impossible for the Ego to assimilate – is found/created and opens up once again to a new opportunity of elaboration (the process of subjectivation). As Balsamo (2009, p. 19, author's translation) reminds us, this *scenic diphasism* implies a 'structural necessity' that, even before human sexual diphasism, characterized by a period of latency between infantile and adult sexuality, lies in the 'difference between perception and representation, between the time in which something happens and in which something is given meaning. In other words, between what has reached the psyche and its possibility for representing this encounter to itself.' This is no less than the starting point of the subjectivation processes.

In music, silence, the void and the pause are all fundamental elements, to the point of constituting gravitational foci for whole musical passages, as in Beethoven's famous incipit to his Fifth Symphony (fig. 1.1), in which the first of four equal chords is replaced by a pause, on which, however, the beat falls.

Something similar occurs in syncopated rhythms, present to varying extents in all musical genres, from the most sophisticated to the most popular, from the oldest to the most contemporary.

Figure 1.1 Ludwig van Beethoven's Symphony No. 5 in C minor, Op. 67: the incipit, with the main accent on the pause.

Despite cinema finding its place among the visual arts, the soundtrack often plays a leading role in giving meaning to the events represented via action and dialogue. One of the many possible examples that struck me while I was writing these notes is in the film *The Kid with a Bike*, by Jean Pierre and Luc Dardenne (2011). Throughout the film, the soundtrack – which mirrors the decision not to overload the plot, in itself dramatic, and representation of the characters with non-essential or melodramatic details – remains in the background, or better, stands out for its absence, or silence. In some particularly significant moments the action stops and then the music powerfully bursts through, never completing a musical phrase, but hanging like a suspended, never-changing sound cell that closes back in on itself without leading to anything, lacking logic, meaning and direction. This sudden emphasis, this violent irruption, this absence of links to anything that came before or will come after and, above all, this ceaseless repetition had an unpleasant and disturbing effect on me. But when the passage returns for the last time to accompany the final scene and then the credits it is no longer interrupted as before: the piano sounds and suddenly it is Beethoven's Piano Concerto No. 5, the 'Emperor' Concerto. It is as though that traumatic nucleus had managed to overcome the raw need to repeat itself unchanged and had opened up to embrace development (and what a development!) that in some way was already present in the cell closed in on itself, but which at the same time gave it meaning anew and allowed the psyche to represent it to itself.

Notes

1 This point is very relevant for psychoanalysis since its therapeutic tools mainly make use of the oral–auditory medium; even training is based primarily on the oral transmission of training analysis and supervisions and does not generally include the use of videos, Powerpoint presentations or other visual technical aids (at least, not before the 2020 Coronavirus pandemic).
2 Thus allowing identification of declarative statements, interrogatives and the like, characterizing different languages or individual styles of expression, and detecting nuances of mood or momentary states of mind, and so on.
3 These, too, characterize individual languages, but also the idiom of each individual, the aims of the communication, the speaker's state of mind…
4 In this context the concept of evolution takes on a more extensive meaning than the classical one, including both biological evolution (Darwin) and cultural evolution, in which acquired characteristics are inherited (Lamarck).
5 Stern (1985) has shed light on how the world experienced by the child is not a world of images, sounds and tactile sensations, but a world of forms, movements, intensities and rhythms, in other words, a world of a-modal qualities, which can be transposed from one mode to another, and which he calls *vitality affects*.
6 The name of the African *djembe* drum seems to derive from *anke dje, anke be*, which, in the language of the Bamana population of Mali, means 'all together in

peace'. The *djembe* plays a key role in the transformative encounter between the main characters in the film *The Visitor* (2008).
7 Although Claude Lévi-Strauss has stated that music, despite being generally considered 'the art of time', is in actual fact 'a machine for the suppression of time' (1964, p. 24). For Kierkegaard (1843a), music is the most abstract expressive medium; it exists only in the moment in which it is played, and sensual immediacy is its object, which language, implying reflection, cannot express.
8 It is also the 'acoustic' scene, and betrays its derivation from that other scene, that of tragedy, whose space–time unit allows catharsis to occur.
9 Upbeat rhythm, with the stress placed on the weak or 'off' beat, contrasting with the downbeat that falls on the strong or 'on' beat, produces the feeling that a vital support is missing, almost a pursuit for stability.

Chapter 2

Listening to the link: Music and primal relationships

> To breathe before saying a word, or playing a note or a phrase, is in itself a proof that silence, or rather a silence, is needed ... the silence of a breath turns out to be the space in which objects, sounds and meanings take up their natural rhythms.
>
> Mario Brunello, Italian cellist and conductor
> (2014, p. 24, author's translation)

Research on the origins of the human psyche leads us to recognize the basic role that musical elements perform in primal experiences, where they operate long before the expected onset of language development. As mentioned in Chapter 1, Susanne Langer (1942) already pointed out the similarity, or rather, the shared nature, between features of inner life and experience on the one hand, and formal properties of musical structure on the other, such as the sequence of motion and rest, of consonance and dissonance, of expectation and satisfaction, of excitement or sudden changes: a primal semantics, or better an 'ur-semantics' (Kühl, 2007). In line with Igor Stravinsky, who argued that music cannot explain anything about emotions, ideas, affects or natural phenomena but can only explain itself, Panksepp and Trevarthen (2009) stress that musical meaning is never dependent on factual reality but is only self-referencing, though always implying emotions as well. Moreover, they regard human musicality as a distinctive motive system (*intrinsic motive pulse*), involving emotional self–other awareness. In their research on the origins of musical experience, while restricting the range of their observation to the human voice pervading mother–infant love duets, they put forward the interesting hypothesis that musical stimuli could modulate the expression of specific genes in the human brain leading to lasting epigenetic transformations.

Within the framework of an evolutionary approach, a more radical hypothesis than Brown's *musilanguage* (Brown, 2000; a more detailed account can be found in Chapter 1) has been proposed by the semiologist

Per Aage Brandt, in the context of his research on the process of hominization: 'Musical practice preceded the symbolic, or intentionally semiotic, message–signalling practices of modern humans' (Brandt, 2009, p. 31), so that language developed out of musical roots. In his opinion, language cannot do without musicality in order to be able to intentionally refer to more complex situations than the factual contents shared by people through communication, and symbolization itself might spring from a primeval human musical activity. Discretization, by which sounds are made discrete elements rather than glissandos, and finitization, whereby rhythmic pulses are turned into parts of finite sequences rather than an endless flow of beats, are fundamental pillars for generating symbolic forms (ibid., p. 42). The fluency we experience in dividing words into syllables might result from the musical link between tones and times, while the syntactic constructing of sentences may possibly be an additional melodic superstructure.[1]

At an ontogenetic level, Anzieu (1979) described the existence of a sound mirror and an audio–phonic skin at the dawning of life, which work together to build up a pre-individual psychic whole or a self–unity. They are the foundations of the processes for acquiring signifying and symbolizing abilities, long before the emergence of visual mirroring phenomena, as highlighted by Winnicott and Lacan. This sound 'skin–self' originates from the sonorous bath in which the baby is suspended since the early structuring of her/his hearing apparatus, between the first and fifth months of intrauterine life. After birth, the sonorous environment is increasingly enriched by sounds that the baby's body produces, thus delimiting a sound space that overlaps with the first spatial–auditory body image, and which is bound to create the early psychic space.

The primal relationship, as appropriately focused on by the sophisticated observation tool devised by Esther Bick (1964) that ultrasound scans have lately dated to the foetal period, is therefore filled with listening and sound-making since the baby's birth, which is, indeed, heralded by the newborn's crying. It was this crying that Freud, in his *Project* (1895), considered the crucial point in which 'a secondary function of the highest importance, that of communication,' appears as a consequence of the substantial asymmetry between infans and adult. The newborn, feeling uncomfortable due to her/his inability to fulfil endogenous urges, can only activate the discharge path, aiming at an internal change; whereas the adult, prompted by the infant's cry demanding that attention be paid to her/his condition, can intervene by changing the external reality (Freud, 1895, p. 317). The hypothesis can be formulated that the experience of a link between the infant's cry and this 'specific action', together with the ensuing activation of the secondary function of communication, is the first step in the process through which the *infans* becomes a subject. Moreover, the experience of listening to oneself as a source of sounds, as well as the proprioceptive perception of one's own movements and bodily positions in space, comes long before the awareness of oneself as a visual object of the other (mirroring).

Neuroimaging research highlights that the human newborn's specific musical competence has its source in definite areas of both hemispheres that can interpret structured sound sequences, mainly those consisting of rhythms matching bodily rhythms. A common neural substrate, originally dealing with the syntactic elaboration of music, would not need to undergo a substantial reorganization in order to also manage language perception and production (Turner and Ioannides, 2009). The wider bilaterality of cerebral substance devoted to music rather than language and the innate ability to be affected by music lead to a consideration of language as a highly specialized subclass of musical cognition.

While listening to her baby is a new experience for the mother, only preceded by perception of its heartbeat or intrauterine noises as registered by diagnostic instruments, the newborn is already a skilled listener with a rich past experience of sounds and rhythms that have by then formed a base for the psychic structures of her/his relationship with the world. Coming from an abode made up of tactile, proprioceptive and acoustic perceptions, muffled by the intrauterine environment, the newborn abruptly comes into contact with a world composed of changing lights and images, significant fluctuations in temperature, movements in the surrounding setting, sounds from the entire frequency range, figures that change shape and move in space ... The baby's first reaction to all this is crying, a forceful ejection of air out of the respiratory tract, thus creating sound vibrations that are welcomed as an index of its good health and strength. Contact with air is another big novelty, which results in the first perception of discontinuity, which was lacking in the liquid world of the motherly womb; air, for the first time, brings the new human being into contact with infinite space and limitlessness.

It should be emphasized that sound waves travel through air space, amplifying the linear and adhesive boundary between self and not-self: in this way, a space is created in which psychic elaboration and transitionality may take place or, in other words, a transition is enabled from bi-dimensionality to tri-dimensionality, which is the difference between the propagation of light (straight lines) and that of sound (three-dimensional waves). Moreover, the bidirectionality of the sound vibrations that make up the sound envelope leads it to acquire a productive function after the receptive one, and thus to be fundamentally implicated in the incipient subjectivation processes.[2]

More specifically, the voice, which long before becoming an instrument and vector of language is already impregnated with rhythm and intonation, makes up the 'embodied' element of sound perception and production. It articulates mind and body, thinking and acting, conscious and unconscious, emotion and meaning. It lends timbre, tone and intonation to the words, thus making up a basic and signifying layer of verbal discourse. Both one's own and the others' voices, through their vibratory qualities, *touch* all the infant's bodily depths and participate in building the tactile–sound envelope that holds and puts the infant in *touch* with the external world. While 'the calling between the mother and the child immediately endows the voice with the quality of a lost object', as an 'echo of a primal absence' (Serra, 2012, pp. 123, 124, author's translation), the voice is also the bearer of a memory as ancient as the conception. Being older than words, it bears the earliest and hidden sensory, musical and affective experiences: 'It is the voice and not only language that opens up access to the unconscious' (Pigozzi, 2008, p. 43, author's translation) and leads to the heart of subjectivity; 'The voice seems to be the word's body or, more precisely, the sexual of the word' (ibid., p. 54, author's translation). Its inherent quality of timbre, which makes the subject's voice recognizable, similar to the unicity of the author's or performer's timbre in musical orchestration and execution, constitutes a basic musical element in family transmission and in the newborn's inscription into the generational chain, both by qualifying her/his voice as specific for a particular family and differentiating it as unique and different from anyone else.

Temporality, music and psychic functioning

Temporality, too, as an indispensable element of subjectivity and symbolizing functions, stems from embodied roots, since it develops from progression, rhythm and pulses of vibrations, sounds and silences that the embryo perceives inside the womb, as well as from its own early movements, which are nothing but changes of position in space and time.[3] Heidegger (1925) wrote that existence (*Dasein*), as understood in its extreme possibility of being, is *time* itself, rather than being *in* time. Time is not outside ourselves, like a pre-existing something to be experienced, but is part and parcel of our nature of bodily beings belonging to a developing reality that is undergoing unceasing transformations: symbolization is tightly intertwined with the unfolding of a subjective temporality.

Music, in its definition of 'the art of sounds in the movement of time' (Busoni, 1922), is therefore inherent in the processes of somato-psychic birth: its essential components of rhythm and melody, as a matter of fact, are parts in a continuum of vibratory phenomena[4] that span the entire range of sound energy and human chronobiology. The spectrum of frequencies that are perceived as pitches blends over, at the lower boundaries of its range, where vibrations can no more be perceived as pitch or sound, into the rhythm frequency spectrum: this reaches approximately from the highest frequency at which it is humanly possible to articulate and perceive rhythms in a coordinated and regular way down to the end of the *rhythmic present*, where individual pulses cannot be perceived anymore as rhythmically correlated. Interestingly, this rhythm window (0.17–20 Hz) includes all the frequencies of human voluntary and involuntary movements,[5] and of neural oscillators such as those which generate alfa (8–12 Hz), beta (>12), delta (<4) and theta (4–7) rhythms, detectable by EEG recordings (Osborne, 2009).

It turns out, therefore, to be inadequate to state that 'rhythmic activity is a basic property of living matter' (Reinberg, 1998, author's translation), whereas it is more appropriate to say that it is music with all its components of rhythm, melody and harmony, including silence as an original and generative element. 'Music allows listening to silence, besides being listened to in silence' (Brunello, 2014, p. 18, author's translation).

According to Busoni (1907): 'That which, within our present-day music, most nearly approaches the essential nature of the art, is the Rest and the Hold (Pause) … The tense silence between two movements – in itself music, in this environment – leaves wider scope for divination than the more determinate, but therefore less elastic, sound' (p. 23). The pause is a metered silence, an expressive and rhythmic void, all the more significant since the accent of the musical phrase may sometimes be located on it (e.g. in the renowned opening bars of Beethoven's Fifth Symphony). The hold or *corona*, on the contrary, is the indefinite, a postponement of the time flow that lets the sound go on *ad libitum*, a musical element that amplifies the sound effect of what comes before, both keeping the meaning of what has preceded and underlining the expectation of what is to follow (figs. 2.1 and 2.2).

As already stated in Chapter 1, breaks and regularities that make up rhythm provide both an experience of continuity and spaces of absence and emptiness: the expectation of repetition, as well as of something new, is what can lead to representation, starting in a tiny dimension the process that leads from absence to symbolization. From this point of view, rhythm might be considered a transitional phenomenon.

Expectation and repetition are essential temporal elements of rhythm that flow into the psychic activity of elaboration and synthesis in which, through the subject, the present expands to comprehend past and future. David Hume suggested that 'repetition changes nothing in the object repeated, but does change something in the mind which contemplates it' (Deleuze, 1968, p. 90). Repetition, which is prone to cause feelings of boredom at a conscious level, gives rise to deep and unknown emotions at each new listening of the same piece of music because it affects the whole somato-psychic realm, from the more aware Ego levels down to the most unfathomable pertaining to the body and the Es.

Figure 2.1 Frédéric Chopin's Prelude in E minor, Op. 28. In the concluding bars, the first corona, on a pause, prepares for the conclusion, while the second lengthens the final chord to an undefined end, up to the performer's discretion.

Figure 2.2 Robert Schumann's Arabeske, Op. 18. Here the corona emphasizes the change in time, as well as in musical idea, rhythm and atmosphere: it creates an expectation that leads back to the first theme.

Expectation is also the time of delay which, according to Freud (1940), allows the Ego to interpolate 'between the demand made by an instinct and the action that satisfies it, the activity of thought' (p. 199): the object absence allows thought and representational activity to emerge. From a more relational point of view, Bion (1965) adds to the object absence the capacity to tolerate the 'no-breast', which becomes available when an adequate maternal *reverie* has set the alpha function in motion, thus protecting the *infans* from a nameless terror. Winnicott (1966) describes how the child, confronted with an absence of the mother that exceeds the time she/he is able to retain her image, cannot use the symbol of union anymore and falls prey to unthinkable anxieties leading to a permanent deformation of psychic functioning and to a failure in developing transitional and symbolic processes. Here we also find a hint at the development of the sense of time and its psychic structuring in two moments, which in this context involve the other's intervention. The newborn's ability to estimate time appears, therefore, to be ontologically tied to her/his ability to build and retain a caregiver's image together with a sense of being one, as well as to her/his compelling somatic needs: the whole thing is included in an inescapable relational dimension.

Laplanche (1999) differentiates perceptual time from inherently human temporalization: the first is the time of immediate consciousness, which is related by Freud to perception and its rhythmicity, and thus pertains to the conscious–preconscious system, that is, to the possibility of creating a historiography. The second is defined by *après-coup*, a translating movement that recovers the past starting from the present while looking forward to a future, whose origin always refers to an internal, unconscious 'other', a remnant from the translation of the external 'other's' enigmatic message.[6] In music, a key element of emotional response depends on movements of anticipation and resolution following one another: such a response becomes more complex when music takes on an unexpected (i.e. other or strange) direction, which can only later be attached to a recognizable meaning, perhaps already implicit in what came earlier (Turner and Ioannides, 2009). Here again we can see a bidirectional move, closely overlapping with the second temporality form as described by Laplanche, and rooted in the alterity of an abrupt or enigmatic gesture. During foetal life, the rhythmic structure of early perceptions – also made up of voids (pauses) delimiting solids, and of unexpected trespassings of sounds (*corona* or *fermata*), which do not allow one to abandon oneself to a foreseeable rhythm – paves the way for the complex temporal structure characterizing unconscious processes, that is, the *après-coup* movement.

Time, in all its elaborated musical articulations, is, therefore, a central element in the subjectivation process, which always goes together with pain and mourning during the shift from primal narcissism to the capacity to be alone in the presence of the other, as well as from the excessive nature of the body and drives (the other inside ourselves resisting transformation and representation) to phantasy production and the development of thought and language, which allow the subject to enter historical time. Music, which unfolds in time, may be considered a materialization of the mourning process as it proceeds through unending transformations and the continuous creation and destruction of sounds that are thereafter replaced by others. Music leaves behind not only silence and void but also the inner transformation of the listener who, by memory and anticipation, integrates its passages so that at the end the external object is no longer there; instead, there is an internal object that enriches the subject's Ego and inner world.

Cosimo, or the subjectivation arrhythmias

At the beginning of the consultation, requested for the child's severe obsessive symptomatology, Cosimo's mother tells me he is 'a child who was born in the middle of conflicts', pointing in fact to the unresolvable oppositions the child is exposed to: daddy and mummy, separated, mutually blaming each other of 'priming' or 'morally subjugating' him; the town where he lives and the other one, where the grandparents have settled, where the mother is always about to move to and from where Cosimo, according to his father, comes back changed every time; the ultimate choice imposed by the father on the mother: 'Or me or your parents', and to Cosimo: 'Or daddy or mummy'. Rather than a rhythmic oscillation similar to a musical and psychic alternation of tension and relaxation, here there are only mutually excluding alternatives that oppose an integrating working-through, apt to generate a transformative and developmental movement. More than discontinuity, which is already a central point in this child's history, the parents' desire appears to be constantly off-centre with respect to Cosimo's birth. His mother defines him as 'the new and the old son', referring to the couple's aborted child, following a shared choice before marriage, which thus represents for both partners their common experience of unloved children. Cosimo's birth is also intertwined with feelings of guilt and expectations of punishment, which led the couple to marry and conceive him, a late unhoped-for 'miracle', and also an attempt at narcissistic reparation that has nothing to do with a desiring impetus. The continual coming and going that informs the *après-coup* time, specific of psychic life, is restricted and stiffened by his parents' unfulfilled needs: the in-presence-child is burdened with the adults' projections, assignments and expectations, while their wounded narcissism makes the boy's narcissism run aground in the bud. The reference to a miracle points out that Cosimo's existence relies on an alien reality, devoid of gravity, in a decentralization that can only generate futile, ineffective movements, like a stripped screw. Unfortunately, this reparation is never sufficient, and Cosimo has to be the 'most loved child in the world' and, subsequently, the one most ardently fought for. He is the guarantor of the constantly sought validation of the couple's parental identity, a verdict that inescapably supplants their desiring attitude. The superlative form dooms this child to loneliness and traps him into an anti-developmental omnipotence.

Dyschrony and dislocation, which have marked Cosimo's conception and birth, initiate his existence from an unthinkable nucleus that cannot allow the generation of a primal rhythm as the source of a sound space in communication with the external world. Cosimo, currently five years old, has retreated into his own self-periphery, taking upon himself the function of border guard (obsessive defences), constantly on the alert because of the danger of explosions (phobia of balloons): he spent many months, at the beginning of analysis, in exploring the environment and the playing material, used only with the aim of classification and with an obsessive attention to putting everything away, as if to erase all traces of his own passage. By absenting himself constantly to go to the bathroom, Cosimo confronts me, in a very concrete transference–countertransference, with the ruptures and gaps his existence is based upon. In such a conjuncture, splitting is a necessity for him, as when he happened to say to his mother, causing great amazement: 'I did my best to get the two of you to split!' Separation has, indeed, no place in the mother's mind other than as a traumatizing and tearing event forced by her son's first separation signals. After a few months, something starts moving: a long series of sessions are spent in preparation for either a play or a representation that there is never time to realize, as a frame or a spatial–temporal envelope for that unthinkable and silent nucleus occupying his self–core, whose existence, however, can now at least be guessed at and sheltered.

After a short time in Cosimo's analysis, I decide to work regularly also with his parents, in order to integrate their personal psychotherapies and provide a support to their son's analysis. Their experience of both his separative and re-approaching efforts, in relation to his visitation and stay schedule, begins to change from a desperate account of Cosimo's rejection – firstly of his father, and then of his maternal grandmother, a significant and often intrusive presence in his relationship with his mother – to their inability to bear Cosimo's pain when moving from one parent to the other; at a later stage, the parents became more and more anxiously worried that the recent improvement in their relationship could raise groundless hopes of their reunification, leading to the child's bewilderment.

While the unforeseeable and frightening noise of blowing up balloons forces Cosimo to avoid any festive situations for children, in the sessions he begins to use his voice to fill everything, without leaving me any space to intervene. Sometimes it is a real 'sound confusional state', which assaults and seizes me because it is unintelligible and obscure, for both the producer and the recipient of the yells, both in its contents and emotional intensity. At other times, by mimicking his father's voice, his teacher's, or mine, or through the puppet Fiocchetta, Cosimo becomes the other, whose pitch and accent, lexical oddities and mistakes and idiosyncratic pet phrases he imitates perfectly. However, it is not really a game, but an act of sheer possession or alienating identification, with absolute prohibition for me to address the boy Cosimo. I find myself plunged into a sound bath devoid of any solacing and holding quality that, on the contrary, violates, paralyzes and annihilates me, constraining any possible creative emergence on my part. Sound and voice have acquired persecutory features; they hurt through their materiality, and they do not allow either an opening out of a transitional space, or the birth of a thought. What is lacking – and what Cosimo had possibly been lacking in infancy – is that pause, or significant void, which Busoni showed to be a key element of music: this specific void, at the origins of the psyche, creates the gap or discontinuity that enables the emergence of a psychic motion and, in a subsequent development, becomes the absence out of which communication and symbol will originate.

Confusion and sound saturation have lately given way to the emergence of a new demand for temporality: Cosimo begins to periodically enquire about the time left in the sessions, discriminating his own time, which is absolute (either infinite or worn out), from mine, which can open up to more flexible horizons. On some occasions he asks whether the session is over, only to add, mimicking my voice: 'Almost!' Playing with characters, Cosimo allows the emotion of astonishment to make an appearance, a feeling that implies an expectation, which in this case is wrong-footing rather than fulfilling.

Only subsequently does Cosimo discover the comforting message that a sound can convey about the other's presence: after two years of therapy he starts reproducing ritually, at the opening of the sessions, a situation of disconnection between viewing and hearing, by asking me not to see the puppet he is using as a spokesperson while I am allowed to hear it approaching from the noise of its steps. Perhaps this dissociation between the senses that are used to give meaning to an encounter reproduces a primal condition in which the phonemic component makes up the basic stimulus of the psychic birth and of the early efforts to decode reality, in a way confirming Anzieu's (1979) statement that the acquisition of prelinguistic meaning (from crying and later on babbling) precedes the emergence of infra-linguistic meaning (from mimics and gestural expressiveness). Robert Schumann himself made Florestano[7] state: 'A good musician understands a piece of music without reading the score, and a score without hearing the music. The ear requires no eye, and the eye no ear' (1970, p. 11, author's translation).

Green (1993) conceptualized negative hallucination as a precondition both for subjectivation and representational functions. To the visual blank described as a product of negative hallucination, I would add silence as a sound void: both of them are expressions of the mother's ability to let the infant negatively hallucinate her, thus laying the foundations for the upcoming representational processes.

In his playing activity Cosimo acts out his own absence, occupied by the overwhelming presence of the interacting characters, for whom he often asks me to give a 'body' but without words. He makes me feel the pain of neither being allowed to utter a sound, while being, on the contrary, dubbed or voiced by someone else, nor being able to address who is in front of me but in fact is not there: might it be a shared negative hallucination? Previously there was the preparation for a party never to be held, then for a performance never to be enacted: now I witness the building of houses that are only made of walls, of vehicles that take nobody anywhere, and of paths made of a sequence of insurmountable difficulties, which again and again are done and undone. The acted absence is always Cosimo's absence, as highlighted by the disappearance or acquired invisibility of many characters, as well as by the intertwining of these themes with postponed or missed sessions because of his parents' engagements or mistakes. One day, while insisting that Cosimo is not here, he adds that he has no session at all today, but tomorrow: while reaffirming his dyschronic existence, he is at the same time letting our minds outline an image of self, which is expected to become representable in a far away, but still possible, future.

Cosimo gradually becomes able to express his ability and wish to invest his own inner world, by asking me to get to know the inside of my home as well as my help in colouring his drawing of the interior of the castle that represents the session room. He also brings a puppet from home into the sessions, which becomes the sister of one of ours, whose name she shares: starting from this redoubling (repetition), being announced long before (expectation), Cosimo ventures into the working out of the infinite possibilities of integration of what is good and what is bad in the others' inner worlds. Good and bad were formerly kept well apart, with all evil ascribed to a pair of male characters, first strictly excluded from his activities, and later on invested with all the bad intentions and actions. He can now get angry at his father who forgot to take him to a session, while through a doll never noticed before he faces gender differences, together with the curiosity and excitation inherent in his overly close relationship with his mother.

Cosimo's relinquishing of omnipotence and splitting matches a progressive relinquishing by his parents of their exclusive position of frustrated and needy children, both envious and competitive, and their beleaguering me with enraged and unlimited demands that always left them unsatisfied while everything they got from me was devalued. Moreover, they can gradually take on dimensions of parenting that thus far were still entrusted to their own parents or to Cosimo himself as well as to me, as a parent to be enviously attacked because endowed with all good possessions: the attitude to contain pain and the ability to think and to instil love and hope (Meltzer and Harris, 1976). The parents' couple can now enlarge the space accorded to Cosimo and relieve him of their projections, letting him move more freely: as the parents begin to feel supported by a gaze and listening that are neither destructive nor engulfing, their gaze and listening become disposed to support their child's feeling of being the subject of his own experience.

This phase of Cosimo's analysis reaches a turning point when, before the summer vacations, Cosimo appears to reset time in motion, by restoring positions in generations and gender roles of the family dolls, so far completely undifferentiated in their genders and kinship ties. Moreover, he announces that a puppet that had before been speaking only an unalterably childish language has eventually learned to pronounce consonants. The sound of my voice, through an acted phone call, succeeds in getting Cosimo to enter the session as a subject. Up to the point that, in the last session before the vacations, he defends his analysis priority from being threatened by the fictitious plan of a new school building in place of the therapy room: he makes a point that, though a school may receive many children rather than one at a time, the aims of the analysis that only the two of us can work at must have top priority.

The music of relationships

Sound, from bodily noises up to the voice, the calling and all the elements of music, plays a key role as a tool of linking with the other in early psychic development, marked by intersubjectivity and the indissolubleness of psyche and soma. Moreover, as music and psychic life are made of the same fabric and dynamics, we cannot do without music in order to approach the earliest psychic motions, as well as the most primitive experiences and functioning. Therefore, in psychoanalytical research we do not need to apply psychoanalysis to music, but music to psychoanalysis.

Research about *motherese*, the language that adults use to address infants, shows that it is its rhythm, melody and prosodic specificity (which instrumental analyses have highlighted) that hold the leading role in fostering mutuality in the primal relationship, through the activation of the infant's social initiative, which in turn gives rise and strengthens parental identity, so feeble and unsure in Cosimo's parents. Even the name that is given to the child is characterized by a rhythmic and phonological specificity, although lacking any conceptual referentiality, since it does not refer to any class of objects but to a singular individual: it is, therefore, semantically arbitrary, but makes the individual a person, a subject included in kinship relationships and heir of transgenerational memories and experiences. 'Proper names should be understood from the point of view of the musicality of personhood' (Brandt, 2009, p. 34);

they embody parental love, the act of giving birth and a specific place in the other's mind and in the group of belonging; they represent a starting point for temporalization and subjectivation processes. The proper name brings along, often unconsciously, the sediments and the somato-psychic traces of experiences and relationships that pre-existed the subject and passed through the parents' unconscious.[8]

The huge implication of sensation and corporality in primal functioning can cause it to be resumed when, as in Cosimo's situation, a new relationship, based upon transference and countertransference processes, and a specific spatial–temporal organization such as the psychoanalytic setting, again sets in motion the oscillation between fusion and discrimination that marks the experiential, representational and communicative wholeness made up of the infant and her/his parents. The expression 'spoken shadow', used by Aulagnier (1975) to refer to the mother's relationship with her unborn child, who needs a specific space for its Ego to be allowed to 'come into being', appears to underline the visual aspect, in a negative form (the *shadow*), as well as the auditory one, in a passive form (*spoken*), both present long before the unfolding of the basic need of the dawning psyche to metabolize the heterogeneous through the early forms of representation. The shadow, just as the corona in music, stands for the spreading of the maternal subjectivity over the child's own, whose gaps and blanks, as rhythmical and musical elements, imply expectation and are designed for convergence into a vital rhythm just centred on the subject. As for Cosimo, gaps and blanks had lost their dynamic quality and became either voids that transformational and re-presentative functions could not recover, or unmetabolizable and occlusive solids.

The analytic setting, as a spatial receptive void, with clear and lively boundaries, and as a temporal structure qualified by a rhythm of its own that intertwines with that of the patient, supports the analyst's interpreter function right at the point when from the affect a word can rise to name it: listening to the relationship can oppose the risk of excess which leads to *secondary violence* (Aulagnier, 1975) and the resulting obstruction of the necessary space for subjectivation.

When we are in the realm of primal processes, the unconscious temporality, never linear, moves no more among repressed, conflictive past representations, but starts from ruptures that cannot be experienced and therefore registered as representations, giving rise to the fear of breakdown as described by Winnicott (1974). This is interpreted by Ogden (2014), rather than as a psychotic breakdown, as a breaking off of the mother–infant tie, leaving the baby alone and on the verge of non-existence, so that she/he is forced to cut off everything that would put her/him in contact with primitive agonies: inherent emotional limitations are thus derived from these unlived aspects of his life. In such circumstances, the analyst's work should consist of just 'helping the patient to live his unlived life in the transference–countertransference' (Ogden, 2014, p. 215). It might then be hypothesized that when ruptures of the dawning sensory organization happen before the possibility of the existence of a mother–infant bond, due to the still prevailing un-differentiation of prenatal unity, they will affect the core of primal processes together with their rhythmical and sound features.

In Cosimo's case, I used the terms *dyschrony* and *dislocation* to qualify a very precocious distortion of the organization of somato-psychic functions that unfold through temporal and spatial processes. In these processes, a key role is played by musical elements in the broadest sense, yet with specific reference to rhythm and melody (both derived by oscillatory phenomena), as well as to harmony and timbre (resulting from the intertwining of sounds of different pitch and quality). The space dimension is present too, particularly if we consider the propagation of sound waves in the environment, which reverberates them in a modified form, thus providing us with basic information for our survival. In the outlined clinical situation, the distortion of the child's psychic structuring processes acquires a primal quality because it is rooted in the parental couple's suffering about the desire that engenders conception: Cosimo, indeed, *comes into being* out of time and place in relation to the first baby generated by the couple, who was probably the child of desire, and has to place himself in a reparative 'after', taking on an unavoidably impossible task. At the same time, the spatial dislocation of his internal processes, as described in the development of both the clinical work and the inherent therapeutic relationship, was initially substantiated by the instability of his environment and of his reference figures.

A quality of listening that is addressed to the relationship and its musical components can, therefore, sensitize us to the perception of events on the border between the psychic and the somatic (Di Benedetto, 2000), as well as to primal processes that include early, prenatal development but are not limited to it, and that make up an important and idiosyncratic nucleus of our own way of being in the world.

Notes

1 According to Brandt (2009), since natural numbers, too, originate as beats either to be filled or to be left empty, the embodied roots of mathematics might be found in the cyclic nature of musical rhythm.
2 In the assembling of the skin envelope too, touching is inextricably linked to being touched but, in this instance, the relationship mainly has a spatial dimension, whereas time is collapsed in a relationship of simultaneity.
3 Language is body movement before it becomes psychic representation, due to the ability, perhaps innate, of trans-modal integration of sensory information.

4 This aspect led to interesting experiments by musicians such as Karlheinz Stockhausen.
5 Such as heartbeats, physiological tremors, hand gestures, speech, infant sucking, sexual intercourse, body sway and breathing.
6 Malloch and Trevarthen (2009) put forward the idea of a virtual 'musical other' who is present in the baby's mind, a companion whose presence becomes alive through the human narration of sound.
7 One of the fictional characters Schumann invented in order to express, in his papers about music critics, different features of his sensitivity and temperament.
8 This sensory and inaccessible nucleus is the name's alien, unconscious core, at the root of the subject's original splitting.

Chapter 3
On imitation

> As you know, I am working on the assumption that our psychical mechanism has come about by a process of stratification: the material present in the shape of memory-traces is from time to time subjected to a rearrangement in accordance with fresh circumstances – is, as it were, transcribed.
> Sigmund Freud (1896). Letter to Fliess, no. 52
>
> There is something in it of Divinity more than the eare discovers.
> Thomas Browne, *Religio Medici*, 1642

As we have seen, the relevance of sound and rhythmic dimensions in psychic structuring is revealed by the consistency of musical dynamics and elements with the primal somato-psychic functioning of the human being in its early (even prenatal) experiences of the other. Among these shared components I would like to address the pivotal role of transcription, imitation, repetition and variation in both the psyche and music: all of them can be considered specific means for dealing with and working through the impingement of otherness and sameness that are met in the outer and inner world.

In 1982, Stuart Feder acknowledged the need to approach the relationship between music and psychoanalysis 'from the point of view of the music itself ... in which the primary data of the music itself is given due consideration' (p. 303). He pointed to the 'possibility that psychoanalysis might be informed by music rather than the opposite; that a study of how affect achieves auditory representation might say something about the nature of the affect itself in mental life' (p. 303). In fact, opposing forces of tension and resolution characterize both music, among other expressive artistic forms, and perception: they provide perception with an expressive quality, namely the capacity to perceive with feeling (Rose, 1993). Only by means of this ability can the primitive organism begin to make decisions about the expected friendliness or hostility of external stimuli.[1] Music isomorphism with the movement of psychic life, rather than with specific mental contents, as stated by Susanne Langer (1951), allows the experience of emotions without qualifying their object or content: music is a symbolic creation that paradoxically represents nothing but itself nor refers to any object that is different from itself; it is an *unconsummated symbol*. Rather than unveiling latent contents, it is a form that unfolds in time, giving expression to the virtual, through a diachronic dimension that is already enclosed in silence. In the words of Langer (1951), it is a *significant form*, very close to Anzieu's (1987) *formal signifier*. According to Nagel (2013), music can be considered the *aural road to the unconscious*.

From formal signifiers to de-signified signifiers

In his formulations about the unconscious, Laplanche (1987) replaces the Freudian thing-presentations as the specific contents of the unconscious with *thing-like presentations*, which do not retain any reference to a content but only represent themselves: they are *de-signified signifiers* that have lost their quality of representation since they represent nothing but themselves. Rejecting the idea of a biological Id, Laplanche maintains that the unconscious originates from the infant's failed translation of compromised messages coming from the caring adult: these messages bear an unconscious, sexual content that is unknown to the bearer him/herself and whose translation will unavoidably leave waste products with a reified and alien materiality. The early repressions or primal repressions are thereby instituted, the contents of which are de-signified signifiers. As a consequence, in Laplanche's formulation, the unconscious is absolutely destructured, with opposites coexisting side by side: there are no laws of logic urging conflicting impulses to undergo annulation, reduction or integration but only compromise formations; not even complexes, such as the Oedipus complex, can inhabit the unconscious. Repression, as the negative side of the enigmatic message translation, leads to dislocation and a failure of temporalization. Psychoanalysis, dealing with the unconscious, is consequently a deconstruction device. May we hypothesize some continuity between the unconscious and musical structure, since raw, elemental, musical components – such as human environmental noises, body sounds and unstructured tones – need to be translated by the rules of musical language, superimposing categories of time, pitch, harmony and expression?

Moreover, just like form and content, signifier and signified lose their differentiation and tend to coincide in music; at the beginning of human experience there is no clear distinction between inside and outside, or self and other, so that the experience mainly involves surfaces and sensoriality. Ogden introduced a *primitive edge of experience*, a primal psychic position that allows a sensory, pre-symbolic, rhythmic and transforming background (*sensory floor*) for all the experiences to come. There is 'no sense of inside and outside or self and other; rather, what is important is the pattern, boundedness, shape, rhythm, texture, hardness, softness, warmth, coldness and so on' (Ogden, 1989a, p. 33): the infant is her/his own sensory experience, and each gap in form, rhythm, symmetry, pressure and so on amounts to a state of not-being and to a formless anxiety. According to Ogden, this way of functioning is at work throughout psychic life, since the *autistic–contiguous position* is the basis on which the other organizations of experience, the depressive and paranoid–schizoid positions, rely. While Ogden focuses mainly on tactile body surfaces, as opposed to Anzieu's inclusion of all sensory channels in the building of the skin-Ego, what is noteworthy is his emphasis on the simultaneous functioning of the three positions, and specifically the relevance of the paranoid–schizoid position in producing rupture, splitting and fragmentation, required for movement and unprecedented structures to develop.

Laplanche emphasizes that the unconscious is the *thing-like other* (*das Andere*) inside me, the repressed remnant of the *person other* (*der Andere*): it *affects me*, just as once I was affected (and seduced) by the person other. Unconscious thing-like-presentations make up an irreducible core and a quintessence of alterity and, accordingly, a promise of reopening to otherness. Similarly, the continuous challenging by the other's enigma is inherent in the transmission of human experience and culture from generation to generation. What Laplanche (1992) specifies as *the primacy of the other*, which demands that psychoanalysis accomplishes the Freudian unfinished Copernican revolution, urges subjects and generations to perform an endless psychic work of translation in order to metabolize and assimilate such alterity: a very similar tool, in music, is transcription, which is used by musicians both as an updating device for their own works, and as an intersubjective transformational means, particularly in the process of receiving and handing down style and musical forms from one generation to the next.

Transcription and creativity

In the years 1713 and 1714, Johann Sebastian Bach, while staying in Weimar at the court of Duke Wilhelm Ernst, transcribed at least nine of Antonio Vivaldi's concertos, three for solo organ (BWV 593–4, 596) and six for solo harpsichord (BWV 972–3, 975–6, 978, 980). It is not known exactly why Bach transcribed these concertos: what is certain is that he was a creative transcriber. His early efforts, as a choirboy in Lüneburg, at copying out the works of established masters had soon developed into free transcriptions. Although he did not introduce any structural change into the original scripts, restricting himself to small alterations for particular musical or practical reasons, 'his rewrites are often imaginative, and his occasional use of bravura passages to fill in rhythmic holes as well as his creative use of various devices to vary repeated passages also add stylistic flair to his transcriptions' (Cheung, 2000, p. 14). The most noticeable transformation is the slowing down of tempo, which I would regard as a mark of his subjectivity, rooted in his own temporalization processes. On the other hand, these transcriptions had a relevant impact on his compositional style and demonstrate how a musician can compose masterpieces not by inventing something totally new, but by assimilating another composer's style and ideas into his own.

And what can we infer from Bach's transcriptions of his own works for different instruments or ensembles, since we believe that an artist's motivations are never merely practical? Many musicians have provided similar examples, such as Mozart's transcriptions of arias from *Don Giovanni* and *Le nozze di Figaro* for small wind ensembles, Beethoven's transcription of his *Grosse Fuge* from string quartet to piano duet, Stravinsky's transcription of the *Rite of Spring* for piano/four hands, and so forth.

Bach's works have, in turn, been widely transcribed or reused by a great number of musicians up to today, starting from an enthusiastic moment of rediscovery in the Romantic period, mainly thanks to Felix Mendelssohn-Bartholdy. Among many other transcribers of Bach we can mention Liszt, Saint-Saëns, Schoenberg, Busoni, Webern, but even the Modern Jazz Quartet and the Swingle Singers. A remarkable example of reuse of Bach's themes is Schumann's *Album for the Young*, which is built on a complex system of thematic relationships, the most dominant source of thematic material being Bach's Chorale, 'Freu dich sehr, O meine Seele', from Cantata BWV 32, *Liebster Jesu, mein Verlangen* (Leipzig, 1726) (figs. 3.1 and 3.2).

Figure 3.1 Johann Sebastian Bach's Chorale 'Freu dich sehr, O meine Seele' (from Cantata BWV 32, Liebster Jesu, mein Verlangen). The theme used by Schumann is recognizable in the higher register.

Figure 3.2 Robert Schumann's Album for the Young, Op. 68.1. Bach's theme in a higher register. 2. Schumann's use and transformations of Bach's theme in the same register. a) 'Chorale': same notes and key but doubled in time. b) 'Humming Song': the key is changed and the theme is by contrary motion. c) 'Soldier's March': transposition up a third and shortened notes with separating pauses. d) 'Melody': contrary motion again and a more varied rhythm with broken chords. e) 'Little Piece': the theme is moved by a half bar, transposed to a higher register and broken by a fifth interval. f) 'Poor Orphan Child': transposition, changed key (minor) and rhythm. g) 'Little Study': same key, different time and rhythm, with the addition of harmonic notes. h) 'Vintage Time': distant key, with the introduction of a tenth interval. i) 'Figured Chorale': again the original theme, highly decorated and in a nearby key.

46 On imitation

No less than sublime is the tragically expressive Adagio of Schumann's Symphony No. 2 in C major, Op. 61 (published in 1847), whose main subject comes from a theme in the first trio sonata of Bach's *Musical Offering* (1747) (figs. 3.3 and 3.4).

Translation or transcription acquires a specific meaning in music, being different among different musicians and musical languages. Just

Figure 3.3 Johann Sebastian Bach's Trio from The Musical Offering, BWV 1079 (Sonata Sopr'il Soggetto Reale).

Figure 3.4 Robert Schumann's Symphony No. 2 in C major, Op. 61: first eight bars for the string section. The similarity is evident to Bach's Trio from The Musical Offering.

as now and again the unconscious mnestic traces, in Freud's words (1896, letter 52 to Fliess of December 6), undergo a re-inscription, in a continuous process of stratification, music has a specific tool for processing both otherness and heritage: according to Goethe, quoted by Freud, heritage must be regained if it is to be owned. Moreover, transcriptions of one's own works by a musician may amount to the same process as Freud pinpointed in psychic life, aimed at finding new meanings and expressions for pre-existing psychic contents. In music, however, we should differentiate transcription from reusing or reproducing themes. Transcription specifically conveys the personal mark of the original author, since it involves a content that is replicated, and a form (container) that is the accomplishment of an active, individual subject, requiring a specific work on her/his part and activating a deep psychic work. As a result, a specific meaning is born for the subject, without losing a substantial link with its original source; at the same time, identification of every single author is allowed through this spontaneous gesture[2] that includes and elaborates a stratification of all the forefathers' gestures. In Bach, the urge to translate the work of others takes on a particular intensity, perhaps related to his precocious orphanage, as well as to his particular interest in reconstructing his own genealogy (Feder, 1993); rather than to parental figures though, he turns to a sort of brotherly zone (Antonio Vivaldi and also Benedetto Marcello and Georg Philipp Telemann, among others). The musical translation of enigmatic signifiers gives birth to unconscious and preconscious elements that make a creative life possible, as well as rooted in the subject's true self.

Paradoxically, the very component of repetition and imitation that is contained in the activity of transcription and/or translation introduces something of the absolute other into the receiver: the pre-existing balance is broken, and a lively core is instated, which can unfold towards unpredictable achievements.

About imitation

Aristotle's theory of art as mimesis, that is, imitation of nature,[3] and specifically of the intrinsic nature of the human spirit, was – up until the late eighteenth century – the basis of Western thought regarding the aptitude of music to express and set in motion affects. According to Aristotle, the extreme variety of harmonies underlying melodies matches all possible different moods, so that listening to their diversity changes our emotional state as well. Such an assumption of a natural and clear consonance between the languages of both sound and affect has for long focused the debate about musical expression on its ability to represent emotional states through sound. Kant, anticipating the spirit of Romanticism, overturned the theory of art as mimesis and maintained that there is no place for rules and imitation in art, since the artist expresses his/her own aesthetic taste in absolute spontaneity and freedom.

Music neither reproduces nor describes reality, which is why it is more arbitrary and less accurate than painting and poetry; at the same time, such arbitrariness and unfaithfulness allow a more sensitive response to musical perception by the human imagination and emotion. The Italian musicologist Enrico Fubini took up Diderot's idea that in music imitation concerns, rather than external reality, a deep, primary, direct and unmediated relationship with the innermost structures of our being and of nature, and with cosmic vitality as well.

Imitation, qualified by Gaddini as 'a disturbance of identification, and with the characteristics of a primitive phenomenon, which probably precedes identification in development' (1969, p. 475), builds up together with repetition the very core of all musical forms, from the most archaic to the most recent, which it permeates with rhythm, melody and harmony.

In 1935, Ralph Kirkpatrick used the sentence by Thomas Browne that I chose as an epigraph for this chapter to express his own admiration for a unique musical work that stirs deep spiritual feelings in listeners and performers: Johann Sebastian Bach's *Goldberg Variations*. Sixty years later, this composition's arcane beauty led Harold Bloom (1994) to term it *uncanny* (*unheimlich*), on trying to approach that unfamiliar, inexpressible and enigmatic sound world, while resting upon a familiar, clear and coherent musical language. The simplicity and greatness of this work by Bach is proved, if ever there is still a need, by the repetition, at the end of the variations, of the opening aria, whose theme, after giving rise to thirty variations, reappears unchanged and leads us to the conclusion: though the notes are exactly the same, and the performer is not requested to play them differently, the climate is transformed and expresses a touching farewell, and a dying away that leads to the closing silence.

Repeating and/or remembering

According to Kierkegaard (1843b), repetition is *a beloved wife of whom one never wearies*, a 'forward recollection' that brings happiness, a spiritual repossession of an endlessly renewed past, not far from eternity. Repetition is new precisely because what is repeated already existed. Similarly, the psychoanalytic concept of *après-coup*, which lies at the core of psychoanalysis, concerning psychosexuality and unconscious functioning, entails a repetition with a latency period: it is embedded in the specific temporality of the human psyche, where time is not linear and continuous but rather discontinuous, travelling in both directions between past and present.

Music, too, is based on both repetition (melodic, rhythmic and structural) and memory of perceived sounds and rhythms that enables us to link them as they are subsequently produced, in an endless work of *après-coup* encompassing the present, the past and the future. Without memory music could not exist; moreover, it is the listening to a melody or a rhythm that reminds us of something already heard that ignites our emotions. Repetition is an inherent feature of music and helps us to discover meaning in the piece of music that we hear or play. Accordingly,

Deleuze (1968) took up Hume's concept that repetition does not entail any change in what is repeated but a transformation in the witnessing mind.

The amount of repetition in music varies enormously, in both qualitative and quantitative terms: more pervasive in folk music as a rule, it depends on the composer's style and inspiration, as well as on cultural traditions, psychic functioning of individuals and groups, instruments of production and reproduction, politics of music production and much more. A musical work originates from the dialectic between similarity and difference, recognition and alienness.

In the classical period, repetitions of entire compositions or their sections had a variety of functions, such as providing balance and unity to the piece of music or allowing listeners to familiarize with totally new musical ideas, which they would not be able to listen to again at will. The *sonata form*, which at the time characterized the sonatas' first movement, is a relevant illustration of repetition. The *exposition* of the two themes is followed by a *cadence* in a new related key: at this point repetition ensures a restatement of the tonic (main) key, perhaps confused or less discernible after listening to the *modulations* (key changes) that connect the two themes. As a result, the two keys are placed in contact and their differences are made explicit: the listener is now prepared to go through the *development* with a more definite feeling of the tonal landscape.

With minimal music, the use of repetition in Western music has attained its most extreme expression. In 1963, John Cage organized the world premiere of a work by the French composer Eric Satie, *Vexations*, written in 1863–64: it basically consists of a theme with two harmonizations on a score covering one page, but with the specification that it has to be played 840 times (fig. 3.5).

The performance lasted eighteen hours and forty-five minutes. Afterwards, Cage remarked that no repetition had sounded the same as the preceding ones, and something had been moved inside him, so that at the end of the performance the world no longer looked the same: a calling into question of the very existence of repetition!

Repetition cannot, therefore, be considered a phenomenon of mechanical and mirror-like reproduction since it involves time, in its occurrence as well as in creating either expectation or a recovering of memory: an early form of psychic or, to put it better, somato-psychic work is thereby set in motion. At the beginning of life, repetition promotes access to symbolization, giving the unrepresented a form that later on will lead to meaning, as Freud illustrated through the renowned wooden reel game. Michel de M'Uzan (1970) differentiates repetition of the same, rooted in the past and memory, ruled by the pleasure principle and therefore endowed with a neurotic quality, from repetition of the identical, within traumatic and actual neuroses: a

Figure 3.5 The complete score of Erik Satie's Vexations.

sterile, excruciating, circular refrain devoid of a temporal dimension and unable to construct a narration of the past in the present. 'It is a good idea to distinguish clearly two types of phenomena among those that, classically, we attribute to the repetition compulsion. Some of these are related to a reproduction of the same and are due to structures in which the category of the "past" has sufficiently developed. The others, which are related to a reproduction of the identical, are due to structures in which this elaboration of the "past" malfunctions' (De M'Uzan, 1970, p. 1211). As a result, the repetition that in 1914 Freud contrasted with remembering and working-through, as an acted memory, was sharply separated from the 1920 repetition compulsion. In addition, coaction to repeat may be further differentiated from repetition compulsion: according to Lambertucci-Mann (2018, p. 21 of her manuscript), the former is a psychic operation that involves some of the Ego functions, whereas the latter develops in the innermost part of the Es, flooding and subjugating the Ego, whose work of deformation and representation fails. Freud described the repetition compulsion as more primal, elementary and pulsional than the pleasure principle; in Green's terms it is to be considered the drive of the drive, an operation aimed at murdering time.

Repetition compulsion, as an indicator of death-drive functioning, may take on an elaborative dimension, when it expresses split and silent elements that were never recognized, listened to and represented (Valdré, 2016). Moreover, the unlinking functioning that characterizes the death drive may be a key element in unlinking a deadly dual fusion and in making new links for new investments available. According to Natalie Zaltzman (1979), death-drive unrepresentability may make way for a *borderline representability*. In this case, it repeats in order to elaborate, and acquires a more vital, rebellious attitude: such an *anarchic drive*, in extreme conditions, may intervene to sustain life.

Linking and unlinking are basic operators of music, accounting for the interplay of predictability and surprise, both embedded in repetition. In music, unlike the other arts, repetition is highly valued: it may be partially compared to the role of main characters in literature, the sentient unitary Ego in poetry, the canvas that hosts and delimits the painting material, the unity of time and place in Greek tragedy or the three-dimensional mass in sculpture, but these similarities cannot cancel the uniqueness of music as far as repetition is concerned. During infancy, we love listening to the same fairy tales over and over again, with the same words and preferably through the same voice, the mother's voice. Similarly, throughout life, we enjoy listening to our well-known favourite pieces of music, without getting tired of them. Repetition becomes part and parcel of music listening: it allows the alternating of anticipation and surprise that makes us feel that we are being played by music, as if we are one with the music that we are listening to and we no longer know whether it comes from outside or inside.

Repetition ranges from being evident in musical works, such as Ravel's *Bolero* or in the identical opening notes of Beethoven's Fifth Symphony (see fig. 1.1), up to the absolute unpredictability of contemporary music by composers such as Stockhausen or Boulez. The almost unbearable dissonance and rhythmic precariousness that characterize the music of these recent authors, as well as the absence of any anchor points, hindering the experience of the *found–created*, produces a sense of alienation, imbalance and bewilderment. In between we find a variety of musical forms and styles that deal with the impossible integration of sameness and otherness: among them, there is the form of variation in which modified repetitions, springing from a single musical idea or theme, and usually of growing complexity follow each other in succession. Variation, often associated with improvisation, was identified as a musical form in the fourteenth century, largely employed in the Baroque and classical periods, and became a structural element of a great deal of jazz music. The theme may be changed in melody, harmony, rhythm, timbre and orchestration. According to Arnold Schoenberg, *developing variation* is a basic compositional principle, lending continuity, logic and unity, as well as contrasts, expression and individuality, to musical works. It is the sonorous expression of psychic work (we might name it *the work of music*) and is the analogue of the psychic function of transformation that Bion profoundly analysed, constantly referring it to the concepts of invariant and O. The invariant is what remains unchanged through transformation; consequently psychoanalysis, rather than unveiling or decoding repressed representations, is concerned with how the mind transforms the emotional experience in order to create meaning (which requires moving the focus from the contained to the container). According to Bion, the zero level of the invariant is the unison, that is, the emotional unconscious experience, originally shared by the infant and her/his mother (*at-one-ment*), from which meaning springs. Transformations, as indicated by the prefix *trans*, may only occur within the encounter of more than one mind.

Music constantly swings between repetition and variation, dealing with a temptation to stop time and the inclination to follow it, between fulfilled and destroyed anticipation, which involves an intensification of emotional tension and, possibly, a surprise effect. In this respect, Michel Imberty (2002) warns us that, when variation exceeds certain limits, the effect of repetition is wiped out, and loss and chaos become pervasive: a failure in the structuring role of repetition results in a painful experience of anxiety and expectancy of the repetition returning. Similarly, Kohut and Levarie (1950) traced music listening and creation back to the Ego struggle to organize the puzzling chaos of sound stimuli.

Imitation: Encountering the other

Imitation needs to be distinguished from repetition, although they are both fundamentals in learning and developmental processes since the very beginning of life. Gabriel Tarde (1890) viewed imitation as a basic phenomenon, both social and physical, ruled by what he outlined as the *laws of imitation* and always intertwined with invention. Jean Piaget (1945, 1947) drew attention to the pivotal role of imitation in the unfolding of symbolic functions and subjectivity, as well as to its being rooted in a primitive and sensory dominated area of experience. He pointed out that whereas imitation in the first month of life is considered a purely reflexive response to external stimuli and in the stage of primary circular reactions (one to four months) is described as indiscernible from repetition, during the pre-operatory stage it becomes *deferred imitation* and results from the baby's ability to mentally represent the actions and behaviours of surrounding people.

While repetition may be confined inside the repeating subject, imitation always implies the other, human or not, and 'installs itself not in the presence of the object but in its absence, and that precisely because of this, its aim seems to be that of re-establishing in a magical and omnipotent way the fusion of the self with the object' (Gaddini, 1969, p. 477). Eugenio Gaddini confers on imitation the feature of being 'one of the earliest identifiable expressions of psychic activity as a whole ... that, moreover, marks the inception of each object relationship' (1968, p. 236, author's translation); at the same time, the wish of *being* the object leads to ruling out the real object and to perceiving it as part of the self.

The connected concepts of *adhesive identification* and *psychic skin* were first described by Esther Bick (1968), who viewed the skin as a primary object, related to the paranoid–schizoid position and the inherent anxieties of falling to pieces and melting away as a formless fluid. When the primary object fails its containing function, skin rashes, verbal production, eye contact or muscular apparatus may become a substituting second skin. Donald Meltzer developed the concept of *adhesive identification* (1975a), which he traced back to a stage when inside and outside are not yet developed: it comes into operation in situations in which the only way for the infant to experience holding is by adhering to the surface of objects. In these junctures, a form of relating develops in which the object is shallowly mimicked: reciprocity, depth and three-dimensionality are lacking, and projection and introjection cannot develop, such as in autistic states (1975b). With the term *adhesive equation*, Frances Tustin (1986) highlighted the fact that the object is not experienced as separate but its surface qualities are assumed as belonging to the individual.

On the other hand, in Ogden's theorization, imitation is an early resource for dawning subjectivity: in the autistic–contiguous position, adjoined sensory and bodily experiences establish pre-symbolic links that provide a sensorial surface from which the earliest sense of self originates. In such a context, imitation may be a valuable defence when the anxiety of dissolution and boundlessness becomes unbearable, involving 'the experience of impending disintegration of one's sensory surface or one's "rhythm of safety" (Tustin, 1986), [and] resulting in the feeling of leaking, dissolving, disappearing or falling into shapeless unbounded space' (Ogden, 1989b, p. 133). Imitation can restore cohesion of the self and the sensory floor for subjective experience, yet it should be clearly distinguished from Winnicott's concept of false-self functioning, since imitation implies neither a within to protect nor a without to conceal. 'Imitation not only serves as a form of perception, defence, and way of "holding on to" (being shaped by) the other, it also serves as an important form of object relatedness in an autistic–contiguous mode' (Ogden, 1989b, p. 136). Autistic–contiguous and depressive organizations merge with their sensory and symbolic modes of functioning, resulting in a complexity that is wider than the sum of its components. A sense of having a place of one's own is generated, together with a potential space in which it is possible to create–discover objects and to feel alive. In conclusion: 'Ogden includes the pre-symbolic domain as pertaining to the varied subjective expressions, thereby distancing himself from the psychoanalytic tradition that tends to equate subjectivity to symbolic capacities ... More than a non-authentic or superficial expression of a psychological organization prevented from symbolizing, imitation reflects here one of the mechanisms that constitute the psychic world' (Salem and Coelho, 2011, p. 136).

With imitation we enter, therefore, into a totally dissimilar field from repetition, imbued with difference and otherness. According to Aulagnier (1975), to live means to endlessly experience what results from a situation of encounter, since the psyche is embedded, right from the start, in a heterogeneous space. Going back to music, imitation is the repetition of a melody by an*other* voice in the context of a polyphonic weave. The restated element differs from the first one through transposition (into a new key), inversion, rhythmic variation, relations between intervals or timbre, while retaining a link with the original sequence. Paradoxically, the ubiquitous presence of imitation in polyphonic Western music turns out to affirm the individuality of single voices. Imitation is not restricted to Renaissance and Baroque polyphonic music: it can be found in the improvisation that characterizes Arabian and Indian vocal music, as well as instrumental and vocal jazz, or, in more predictable forms, in pop music.

The link that Gaddini (1969) emphasizes between imitation and perception, with the expression 'imitating in order to perceive', is very pertinent to music, as well as 'perceiving in order to be', that is, through the bodily changes caused by the encounter with the object. In the same way as these experiences occur in the absence of Ego boundaries, as Gaddini points out, music is an experience positioned between psychic and somatic borders (Di Benedetto, 2000), and activates many sensorimotor channels both in the musician and the listener, up to the point of feeling one with the music. Temporality, which is a core component of music, opening up to the new and the predictable as well, is also implied by Gaddini when he speaks of an *imitative process*, with effects on motor development in infancy. He adds that this sharing of perception and imitation may be the initiator of the differentiation between perception and memory systems, which are, indeed, essential for the very existence of a musical discourse.

Goldberg variations

Johann Sebastian Bach composed the *Goldberg Variations* between 1739 and 1740. A well-known anecdote recounts that the name 'Goldberg', by which this work is traditionally named, refers to a young house-musician employed by Count Keyserlingk. The count, who suffered from insomnia, asked Bach to compose a series of gentle and merry enough works for Goldberg to play to him through the dark hours, in order to relieve his sleepless nights. So Bach came up with the idea of composing variations, a genre that he had always considered a thankless task, as it was grounded in a harmony that is always the same. The *Goldberg Variations*, which performers view as a final accomplishment, is a voluminous and complex composition, constructed with a familiar lexicon but in an entirely personal and unmistakable language. As for the instrument for which it is intended, it appears to have been the average harpsichord available at the time, but there are reasons to speculate it could even have been the fortepiano, which had appeared a few years earlier and was already known to Bach.

One among the proposed hypotheses about the compositional history of the work views, as its original nucleus, the nine canons that regularly come in succession every three pieces and together constitute a sequence from the first canon at the unison up to the last one at the ninth. The canon,[4] which is the most appropriate musical form for pure imitation, is therefore supposed to lie at the core of the variations. The inception from the canon at unison echoes Bion's idea that meaning originates from the unison between mother and infant. The whole set of variations deviates from the classical concept of variations: in the *Goldberg Variations* we cannot find a proper theme, enunciated at the opening, then gradually transformed and developed through the use of passing and grace notes, rhythmic or harmonic changes, ornamentations, rhythmic or harmonic variations. The connection between the opening aria and the following thirty variations lies in the harmonic pattern of the chords, which descends from a widely used cell at that time, while the variations assume broadly different musical forms, according to a well-articulated schema: by means of an unprecedented creative gesture, Bach's aim appears to lie in creating new, unknown music through well-known musical elements (fig. 3.6).

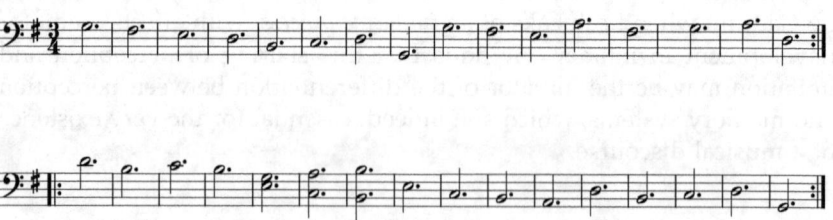

Figure 3.6 The bass in the Goldberg Variations, BWV 988: it covers the thirty-two bars that constitute all the thirty-two pieces of the work.

The bass, which functions as a support for the harmonic framework from which the melody unfolds, in this case takes on an unusual melodic quality and gives rise to extremely disparate variations. 'Just as the *Goldberg* takes an old theme and extends it further, so it takes this principle of "difference" farther and produces a full genre-mix, moving from one strongly characterized and independent variation to another. There was really no precedent for this, common though it has since become' (Williams, 2001, p. 39).

The compositional plan might appear more complex than it was in the composer's intention. As considered through listening, the impression is of a sequence of changes and contrasts: repeated moments of climax alternate with painfully expressive movements, up to the excitation of the last variations, which fades as the opening aria is repeated and brings the work to an end in an introverted and thoughtful mood. Considered from the point of view of its conceptual framework, the work appears to be more static, divided into ten groups of three movements with similar features: a dance or a piece of a specific genre (e.g. a *fughetta*), followed by a brilliant movement made of arabesques that require the performer to cross his hands, and lastly a canon, each time differently structured, according to a sequence of growing intervals, from the unison to the ninth. There are, however, two significant exceptions, within the first and the last groups, a symmetric asymmetry that might have been purposely introduced by the author in order to rupture the listener's expectation of regularity.

The allure of symmetry can also be found in the binary structure of movements, which unfold according to multiples of two: starting from thirty-two bars making up each movement, broken down into elements of eight, four and two bars, up to the thirty-two pieces that compose the whole work, even though a certain overlapping of themes adds an elusive feature to the predictable phraseology based on two, four or eight bars. In the whole, through differing symmetries that rest upon two or three, apparent to the ear and the eye as well, we discover extensive compositional freedom and imagination, not so obvious in a composer such as Bach and, despite a basically contrapuntal structure, an invitation to play *cantabile*.

Imitation in the functioning of psyche and music

As we have seen, repetition, imitation and variation are very different processes that underpin musical development, both within the individual piece of music and in the history of music, through the flowing of musical forms and styles from generation to generation. According to Gaddini, 'imitation is the attempt to master a too intense stimulus' (1968, p. 255, author's translation) by becoming the object: perhaps an early form of the work of the negative, which is also involved in the creation and fruition of music (see Chapter 4). The function of imitation in music shows how the same process may result in the most obvious predictability as well as in the most creative forms of expression, due to its position on the border between sameness and otherness.

'Imitations and introjections,' Gaddini reminds us, 'more or less evolved, remain continuously active' (1969, p. 478), and from the beginning they deal exclusively with animate objects. Making up the basic building blocks for assembling both the psyche and all musical productions, imitation perhaps can only be compared to the originary process, the opening encounter between the psyche and the other, marked by the self-generation postulate: the *pictogram*, the self-referencing representational form in which otherness is at the same time recognized and denied, includes the body of the subject in the image of the object, which is exactly what happens during prenatal life in the encounter between the foetus and the sound object.

Starting from theorizing an imitative functioning that does not require any organized psychic structure (Gaddini, 1977), aimed at restoring the state of the primary self, Gaddini then changed his point of view to consider imitation as the founding of the creative unfolding of the self in the early months of life, which maintains its key involvement in creative processes throughout life, especially in artistic expression.

Notes

1 The same process was put forward by Freud in 1925 (*Negation*) as the primordial mechanism that separates the good inside from the bad outside, at the origins of the psycho-somatic organismic unit: 'The original pleasure-driven ego wants to introject into itself everything that is good and to eject from itself everything that is bad. What is bad, what is alien to the ego, and what is external are, to begin with, identical' (1925b, p. 237). This is the attributive judgement that, according to Freud, precedes the judgement of existence: both make up the function of thinking.
2 According to Arnold Schoenberg (1975): 'Every man has fingerprints of his own, and every craftsman's hand has its personality; out of such subjectivity grow the traits which comprise the style of the finished product ... Style is the quality of a work and is based on natural conditions, expressing him who produced it' (pp. 120–121).
3 Imitation in the sense of representation rather than copying, which in Plato was imitation of imitation, since the concrete world is an imitation of the ideal world.
4 The canon is a musical form in which a first voice exposes a melody that is imitated in succession by other voices at the distance of any interval, such as a unison, second, third and so on.

Chapter 4

The music is not in the notes ... Intimacy and the negative in music

In his book *De l'intime. Loin de bruyant Amour* (Intimacy: Far from Noisy Love), François Jullien (2013) advances insightful considerations about intimacy: 'intimate' stands for both the subject's most inward, hidden and protected part and for the relationship, what is *in-between*. Jullien contrasts intimacy with love, which objectifies and consumes, and its noisiness. According to him, intimacy implies a significant contradiction, meaning both the innermost and the secret in us and the relationship with the other; depth as well as openness to the other. Jullien remarks that intimacy is allowed by the absence of aims and projects involving the other, as is the case in love relationships: there are neither expectations and goals nor anything to be gained. Rather than the lover's desire to conquer a space inside the other, intimacy means unsealing our boundaries to make room for the other and the assembling of a 'we'.

Nevertheless, intimacy remains an enigmatic concept: *intimate* is a superlative, which also entails, if we look at its Latin etymology, the opposite *extremus* and the related verb *intimo*, which means to let in or force into, to make known or penetrate, that is, to intimate!

The absence of objects in the intimacy relationship hints at a specific form of expression, music, whose nature is that of a symbol without a symbolized content. Defined as pure sound and the motion of tonal forms, an empty signifier, by Hanslick (1854), and as a tonal analogue of psychic emotional life, as a significant form or unconsummated symbol, by Langer (1942), music entails the effacement of the opposition of signifier and signified. Di Benedetto's *unsaturated symbol* and Anzieu's *formal signifiers*, as well as Laplanche's *de-signified signifier*, convey very similar conceptualizations.

The essence of music, defined as the art of sounds in the movement of time, lies in it occurring in time and being made of relationships between different sounds, so that it can be found just in-between them. Motion and rhythm, which in the previous chapters I identified as primal elements in the birth of the psyche, might also be at the roots of intimacy.

Moreover, music shares with intimacy the act of being a gateway between otherness and sameness, touching our sensorial apparatus at more than one entry point: not only the ear but also all bodily surfaces on which sound vibrations are perceived. Therefore, music creates a much more pervasive and extensive experience than any other artistic form.

Music, temporality and mourning

Time is, therefore, a key component of music. In this regard, it is worth recalling Freud's 1896 letter to Fliess (no. 52 of 6 December), in which he advances the hypothesis that the psychic apparatus sets itself up from the earliest perceptive traces (*Wahrnehmungszeichen*) by means of successive translations: the important point is that whereas the early perceptive inscriptions are connected by simultaneity associations (e.g. beta elements, pictograms, formal signifiers, source–objects of the drive, etc.), subsequent inscriptions are marked by causality relationships and conceptual memories, as if the birth of temporality has to be identified in this shift. These perceptive traces or signs, which Freud put at the beginning of the psychic apparatus, entail recognizing a sensoriality that, through the repetition of experiences, soon becomes rhythm: this is made up of tension and calm repose, contacts and gaps; these are feeling-signs, immemorial traces of rhythm, an umbilical scar that all human beings owe to the mother function (Balestriere, 1998). Between 1920 and 1925, Freud traces time origins in an undecidable boundary area between Ego, unconscious and sensorial reality. He conjectures that discontinuous functioning of the P-C system gives rise to time representation. What is certain is that the experience of feeling cannot but unfold in a 'becoming', which is itself time. The constancy principle would underlie this swing between tension and appeasement, as well as between pushing towards contact and contact extinction, resulting in the typical rhythm of each individual psyche. According to Balestriere (1998), the abstract representation of time does not result from thinking, but derives altogether from the P-C system working method, and from its own self-perception.

Freud (1920) adds a very intriguing remark: that this way of functioning could work as an additional protective means against stimuli. Time representation would thereby be a protective shield against stimuli. His implication of rhythm, in the succession of opening and closing to the outer world, and his hint at pauses that make it possible to elaborate and metabolize the stimuli, give the impression that Freud had in mind a subjective temporality, rather than either a merely phenomenological time or a form of temporality related to all living organisms, as Laplanche suggests. Rhythm adds to chronological, cosmic time the opportunity to take up the chance, or the event, thus making them metabolizable and historicizable: it is the human being, through a movement of active temporalization, who produces or creates his own time, but always with the other's contribution. I will return to this function of metabolizing the excess when dealing with the work of the negative.

At the beginning of the sense of time, therefore, we find both permanence, which is the certainty of what Winnicott defined as *continuity of being*, and discontinuity, brought about by the event, through the opposition between presence and absence. Ruptures and continuity are core elements of rhythm, each one giving way to the other: absence thereby leads to symbolization passing through the dynamic void of expectancy, which is the realm of the formless and of motion.

The subject's temporality pervades the most idiosyncratic nucleus and the specific modality of somato-psychic functioning, which are different in each individual's personality: it is rooted in intrauterine life, before an external world can be recognized, in the internal–external environment of the womb, brimming with both the mother's and the unborn's sounds and rhythms. From these primal rhythms the subject's temporalization processes and related self-historicization function develop. In mother–baby exchanges the temporal structure is more important than the sensory channel that is used: auditive, visual, tactile, olfactive or kinaesthetic. Starting from such mutual interchange a joint rhythm can unfold, which results from both fulfilled expectations and surprises, and is therefore something new. Such basic rhythm, born inside the relationship with the other, imbues the spontaneous gesture that Winnicott spoke about, and is, therefore, what makes each individual unique.

From a temporal point of view, music is a full-strength expression of the work of mourning, which is embedded in time, in its subjective articulation that is temporality, and gradually unfolds by releasing one link at a time with the lost object. Music, too, is intertwined with time flowing, as it occurs through an uninterrupted overcoming of an element by the subsequent one. This alternation between creation and destruction needs the work of memory in order to grant contour and sense to the sound and silence flow.

Freud repeatedly confronted the enigma of mourning as a process centred on time but, at the same time, never fully solvable: 'Mourning is a great riddle, one of those phenomena which cannot themselves be explained but to which other obscurities can be traced back' (Freud, 1915, p. 306). On the one hand, he writes: 'When it has renounced everything that has been lost, then it has consumed itself, and our libido is once more free … to replace the lost objects by fresh ones equally or still more precious' (ibid., p. 307); but on the other, in 1929, he writes to Biswanger, struck by his own son's loss: 'No matter what may fill the gap, even if it be filled completely, it nevertheless remains something else. And actually this is how it should be. It is the only way of perpetuating that love which we do not want to relinquish' (Freud, 1929, p. 386).

Music and the work of the negative

In addition to the protective function that Freud bestowed on the intermittent way of working of the P-C system, Green (1993) introduced the concept of *the negative* as a specific mode of psychic work, aimed at lessening the excess of excitation and drive energies that otherwise would be unbearable: this concept is of great help in conceptualizing some of the qualities that make music work just as the psyche does, due to its isomorphic nature to psychic life. Laplanche (1989), too, highlighted that the Ego of the *Project*, rather than being identified by its perceiving function (as it will be for the Ego agent, specifically in Freud's writings in the 1920s), is considered mainly for its inhibiting function: the Ego is entrusted with the removal of the excess of inner pulsional excitation, with the aim of clearing the path for the reality index that springs from perception. To continue with Laplanche, the adult unknowingly addresses compromised messages to the *infans* the resulting drive assault requires the *infans* to activate a work of translation that produces children's sexual theories. The failure of this work of translation gives way to repression and the establishment of the unconscious (made of thing-presentations or de-signified signifiers, *drive source–object*): the latter continues to exert pressure both originating derivatives of different sorts and as a remnant to be endlessly translated.

Green (1993) highlights, as a basic necessity in Freud's thought, that something must remain unknown to the subject: desire in the first topic and defence in the second, resulting in a structural negativity. This lack is what makes psychoanalytical theory, since its inception, a theory of the negative. The negative becomes, therefore, the original state of psychic elaboration that, starting from the radical positivization of the drive, arrives at neurotic functioning, which, indeed, Freud defined as the negative of perversion.

Besides the *unconscious*, a key concept of psychoanalysis, in his formulation of the *negative* Green embraces the group of primary defences that deal with excitations and stimuli of inner (*repression*) or outer (*rejection, disavowal*) origin at different levels (e.g. linguistic, in the *negation*, or representational in *repression*) by a yes or a no: Green specifies that forclusion refuses the drive; splitting and denial refuse perception; repression refuses representation and affect; negation refuses the word-presentation. To these basic defence mechanisms, Green adds significant processes of psychic functioning, such as identification and sublimation, as well as, going through the judgement of attribution and the judgement of existence (Freud, 1925b), the disorganizing operation of the death drive or what Green names 'disobjectalizing function'.

Drive excess referred to by Green and Laplanche, ascribed to infantile sexuality (Laplanche's *sexuale*) and qualified by its perverse, polymorphous features, without any fixed aim or object, can be similarly recognized in musical patterns that, in all types of music, unfold through tensions and rests, as well as in the ability of music to mobilize all sorts of affects and somatic sensations: music seduces by entering through an exposed, non-adjustable, *hilflos* sensory organ and, what is more, it touches the body and arouses vibrations that ignore directionality and borders between inner and outer, almost turning the body into a musical instrument. Intimacy may be an apt definition for the encounter and merging experiences opened by the sharing of music, both in performers and listeners.

Among the several meanings of the term *negative* that Green reviews, two are, more than pertinent to music, specific to its essence: the first refers to something that goes on existing in a state of latency, even when it is not perceptible any longer or not yet, or whose existence can be assumed as virtual before it surfaces through perception. Memory of the past and expectation of the future link together this sequence of presence–latency, which are the synchronic and diachronic aspects of music and the negative. The second refers to a *nothing*, something that has never achieved the condition of existence or points to its extinction: in music the most apparent form of this meaning is not only a silence or pause but also phrasing and breathing. In this respect, Green makes his own Bion's distinction between *nothing*, which is nil or the absolute void, and *no-thing*, the not-thing or the absence of thing: a mutilating loss the former, as a result of a double denial of the failed expected satisfaction and of the evacuation of frustration, which is the destructuring component of the negative; a lack, the latter, yet open to different solutions, including representation, which allows the object to be retained when it is no longer available. This last is the structuring form of the negative, also recognizable in music, formulated by Winnicott through the concept of a transitional object: neither *me* nor *not-me*, neither inside nor outside. Freud (1925b) had already pointed out the conservative side of negation, viewed as a means of becoming aware of what is repressed, as it is already a lifting of the repression.

The negative, however, cannot be immediately grasped by consciousness, which is caught by its inherent positivity and has no language to take possession of the negative: because of its connections to drive, the negative has the implacable hardness of repetition coaction, yet it is radically alien to the essence of positivity, characterized by immutability and invariance. According to Green, the negative takes up its meaning in relation to the pre-existing positive, which in fact ignores this unveiled meaning. It is the negative that retroactively confers a sense to the pre-existing positive, as the experience of a lack of existence of what is qualified as positive allows the unfolding of what could not be. It seems, therefore, that the negative lies between the ephemeral of what cannot be grasped and the perpetuity of an unreachable, resistant nucleus, opposing any possible knowledge through mere positivity.

The negative in music

All the above is in accordance with music's structure and dynamics, which are made up of an uninterrupted motion of both audible and inaudible sounds, rhythms and silences, each one implying negation of the earlier ones, and of an unceasing transition from a perceptible present to a past to be more or less recollected and integrated. Together, they bring about expectations that may be either fulfilled or unsuccessful, distorted, diverted, but always going through an activity of unlinking and re-linking, along a path through continuity and ruptures, sounds and silences, consonances and dissonances, rhythms and breaths.

Silence is both the required background from which music arises, and an essential component of its structure. Similar to the concept of negative hallucination, it is a representation of the absence of representation and a framing function for representation. Green (1993) reminds us that an articulate thought is only possible in discontinuity, as this articulating discontinuity implies the void that underlies all thinking chains. The same can be said of music, if we move from visual to sound, and if we refer to musical thinking. As I already mentioned, discontinuity in early rhythm and sound experiences may be exactly what originates psychic life and its movements.

If we consider music as issuing from a selection of sound elements from the totality of thunderous noise made by the uninterrupted and simultaneous production of all sounds and noises, we individuate a work of the negative at its basis: this is accomplished both diachronically, as individual sounds or chords are continuously replaced by others, and synchronically, because only a few sounds are admitted among the whole, as a result of harmonic rules and the author's creative needs as well. The key, for example, is born from priority bestowed to specific sounds above others, on the basis of the tonic or keynote, which is the fulcrum of the musical discourse's development and is the note that names the key. According to Kohut and Levarie (1950), it is the Ego's work to organize and transform into knowable patterns the totality of sounds, allowing pleasure to replace anxiety.

A further illustration of the negative in music is the introduction of the tempered scale (Andreas Werkmeister, 1691), which aimed at limiting the spectrum of sound by cutting down all the possible frequencies within the semitone interval or, in other words, by equalizing the descending semitone from a note to the ascending semitone of the lower one. The natural scale was formerly determined on mathematical foundations, on the basis of frequency ratios and from the acoustic phenomenon of the harmonics, that is, the higher sounds that are produced when a note plays. When a vibrant body (a string, an air column or a vocal cord) generates a sound, it is never pure, but is composed of a mixture of the first sound with higher and milder ones: these natural harmonics are sequences of sounds with frequencies that are multiple of the basic, *fundamental* note, and affect the timbre of each instrument and the definition of keys and their inherent chords. In the tempered scale, mathematical ratios between different scale degrees were changed in order to conventionally remove dissonances that used to make playing together fixed tuning instruments (i.e. harpsichord, pipe organ) and not fixed (i.e. string instruments) problematic: modern harmony was thereby definitively established. On the basis of this negative operation, Bach built his *Well-Tempered Clavier*, two collections (1722, 1744) of twenty-four preludes and fugues in all the major and minor keys: a deeply musical synthesis of the contrapuntal principle of imitation and of the harmonic mechanism of modulation (Mila, 1963).

Another negative phenomenon, which appears to be of an opposite nature, is the progressive dissolution of the key that, starting from musical romanticism, and going through the ultimate Wagnerian extensions, leads to atonality, where reference points are given up and each note is given equal rank – even though the law of sequences (in dodecaphonic music) conveys an indomitable need for order and rules.

The constituent alterity of the human being matches the alterity of music, which works by a continuous appropriation and reworking of pre-existing material: through the author's style, this alterity is transformed and becomes part and parcel of his/her compositional and performing style, a creative outcome born from a deeply intimate relationship between two musicians through their pieces of music. Green's definition of identification as the response of negativity to alterity (1993) appears to be relevant to this regard: while in *Group Psychology and the Analysis of the Ego* (1921) Freud defined identification with the father as a wish both to resemble and substitute the object, Green adds that through identification the Ego becomes the object, while not relinquishing to keep it sequestrated. This involves the risk of undergoing an alienation that undoes one's own subjectivity.

In music this undoing or unlinking, as an expression of the death drive, is flanked by the work of linking in time (melody) and space (harmony). Bio-anthropological research, indeed, shows that in human evolution music has always been a cohesive, coordinating and cooperating tool among individuals and groups, before language development and with a selective advantage for surviving. Moreover, while language follows a horizontal path and needs an alternation of statements, music is endowed with two more vertical dimensions, that is, harmony and rhythm, which facilitate emotional coordination and sharing, perhaps as a result of group selection. This particular way of functioning contributes to the birth and unfolding of feelings of intimacy between people, starting from the earliest, dual, mother–infant relationship.

In the patient–analyst relationship, a specific sensitivity enables the analyst to *palpate* the patient's psychic surface (Kahn, 2012). On the other hand, paradoxically, it is the analyst's attitude as a stranger, namely devoid of the possessive features of love, in front of a fellow man that allows the basic lag that makes motion and play possible. In this regard, Fédida (1995) suggests that this position of *étrangeté*, or being unfamiliar, in which the analyst listens to his/her patient, rather than touching the object as vision does, fosters the gap between the object and its representation: interpretation may only be created within this gap, therefore it is not another meaning but rather a 'between-two-meanings'.

In-between: Music and intimacy

Since the beginning of mankind, music has been considered a powerful inducer of emotions, as if its element of motion is at the same time an affective motor, though it is about feelings without an object and often even without a name. Understanding why a single piece of music or a specific musical passage is able to stir a specific emotion is a very complex problem. Often tonalities are associated with particular moods: the easiest occurrence is the difference between major and minor keys, which everybody can link to very different affective states. Intervals,[1] too, which link or separate the individual notes of melodies, have been used by composers to convey specific affective meanings. An example of this is the *lament cry*: since madrigals in the sixteenth century, moans were expressed through descendent intervals of a second, either major or minor, which we can find in very different composers, from Monteverdi to Verdi, Wagner and Bartok. The interval of a minor second assembles the minor chord of a second, that is, the most dissonant among bichords: thus it becomes understandable why, when the two component notes are played in sequence, they evoke very anguished and unsettling feelings (fig. 4.1).

Figure 4.1 Giuseppe Verdi's Don Carlos, Third Act, Introduction, bars 9–15. The cellos play broken chords that begin by descending minor seconds, while in the lower register we hear acciaccaturas of ascending minor seconds.

The *lament bass* and the *chromatic fourth* are sequences of descendent notes, via minor and major seconds, which are used to represent and induce feelings of sorrow and despair. A compelling illustration of the use of the chromatic fourth is to be found in Bach's *Goldberg Variations*, No. 25: an 'unconventionally conventional' (Williams, 2001, p. 82) harmony offers a life of its own to the accompaniment, and a suffering intensity is achieved through a concentration of the chromatic fourth in both sound registers. 'Such concentration of the Chromatic Fourth is not only exceptional but conceived to be as stirring in its rising form as lugubrious in its falling' (ibid., p. 83) (fig. 4.2).

Intervals, or gaps, therefore, perform a key function in the process of affect signification; we can assume that the same occurs in intimacy, positioned by Jullien (2013) in the in-between of subjects. I think that resonance and co-vibration of similar idiosyncratic elements allow the unfolding of a relationship of intimacy, regardless of contents and aims. Even without a clear content and well-defined goals, intimacy creates very strong links among subjects and opens their boundaries to alterity and strangeness. Exploring how music functions may help us to

Figure 4.2 Johann Sebastian Bach's Goldberg Variations, No. 25. a) Original score of the first four bars: the theme begins with an ascending sixth, that then alternates with a descending chromatic fourth: the result is deeply dramatic and sorrowful. b) Bars 1–4: basso descending chromatic fourth that supports the higher register theme. c) Bars 9–16: tenor and bass chromatic fourths overlapping in the two voice ranges.

understand widespread psychic processes, such as intimacy. Whereas many authors, such as Feder, Rose and Nagel, inspired by Susanne Langer's thinking, have suggested that music mirrors mental life, I attempt to show that it is made up of the same mechanisms as psychic activity, and has a basic function in the very origins of psychic life and unconscious functioning.

Negative listening

Not only do I believe that the psyche works by means of musical forms and motions but also that analytic listening, if we look beyond contents and language, has much in common with musical listening: as an *unconsummated symbol* or *significant form* (Langer, 1942, 1951), centred on silence or absence, music also requires a de-signifying listening. Psychoanalytic listening articulates the analyst's unconscious sensitivity with the palpable quality of the patient's psychic productions in order to encounter the raw material of the patient's word (Kahn, 2012). As a result, through the voice, with its components of timbre, melody and breathing, which inscribe it into one single body and also into a genealogy of bodies, the contact reopens with the infantile sexual, registered as tracks or signs. According to Kahn (2012), voice and presence are repositories of an earlier experience than the signs and images that obliterated and lost it.

The substance of words contrasts, in fact, with what we name clinical material, which through the discourse moves towards a meaningful synthesis aimed to cover rather than unveil. The analyst's body comes into contact with the patient's expressions and the specific psychic materiality of each word, resulting from its contact with the primitive, by becoming a receptive surface endowed with a differential sensitivity. According to Vincent Estellon, 'the psychoanalyst ... auscultates, rather than the patient's body, the body of the words in the patient's words' (2007, p. 182, author's translation).

Musical listening, in turn, is a passive listening due to the physical un-adjustability of the sound inflow, as well as an active listening because it rests on a ceaseless work of linking and unlinking, and signification and de-signification. It is, therefore, a process of creative building that ensues from the encounter of listener and musical object; moreover, when we listen to music we perceive the performer's body contact with the material in which the instrument is made, just like, according to Kahn (2012), the psychoanalyst *palpates* the analysand's psychic skin. Music apparently reaches us from the outside, but listening to music requires a specific concentration on ourselves, exactly the same as what we experience when listening to our patients. This kind of listening might be attributed to an intimate relationship between unconsciouses, which bypasses conscious communication and whereby each subject opens to the other, all the more so as they appear to be alien or absolutely unknown to each other. Moreover, these qualities of musical listening make it very close to a regredient mode of listening that, according to César and Sara Botella (2001), is characterized by an endopsychic attitude oriented towards sensory and hallucinatory experiences, and has a transformative function that can make deeply inaccessible psychic areas representable. Music listening introduces the listener to a void of sense that starts associations and psychic movements on his/her part, as well as sensory memories and hallucinatory phenomena.

I think we can agree with Mozart, if it is true that he said:

'The music is not in the notes, but in the silence between'.

To which Miles Davis added:

'The real music is the silence and all the notes are only framing this silence'.

Note

1 In music, an interval is the difference between two pitches, and may be horizontal, linear or melodic if it refers to successively sounding tones, such as two adjacent pitches in a melody, and vertical or harmonic if it pertains to simultaneously sounding tones, such as in a chord.

Chapter 5
Beyond space, time

The basic concepts of psychoanalysis, and consequentially its practice, have undergone significant transformations over time. Freud outlined two successive topical models of the psyche, to which Kaës added a third topic involving an intersubjective and groupal unconscious, hence ectopic. Pichon-Rivière (1971) formerly introduced the concept of *vinculo*, the third co-built element in the relationship between subjects, and individuated horizontal and vertical links within groups. The concept of transpersonal defences, too, breaks the organized geometry of subject and object relationships, as a result of its blurring of limits and spaces. Thus we arrive at the major changes of setting that consider the partner in the couple, rather than as a mere object, an active subject within the therapeutic relationship, while in family therapies all the members are speaking, representing and acting subjects that share an increasingly complex setting whereby the therapeutic function is not always the exclusive prerogative of the analyst.

The family, like the couple, requires not only an extension in space of the psychoanalytic method but also a temporal extension, as it is a group with a specific history that far pre-dates its stepping into the analytic office; moreover, this history originated long before the family members were born, in the inter- and transgenerational. As a result, in the analytic situation the history is no longer just referred, but occurs in the actual time of the session, since it is inscribed in each member's psyche and circulates with its countless versions through their communications and interactions. In the Z family, who I will address extensively below, since the beginning there is a contraposition between the 'official' history–anamnesis that is presented, focusing pathology and suffering on a single member and a limited period of time, and the several histories that gradually unfold throughout the analytic work: these had never been told before because they were made of shared facts buried in a past in which death threats overwhelmed the family members, forcing them to continually protect themselves.

Freud repeatedly represented psychoanalysis through the archaeological metaphor, which refers to the importance of remembering, repeating and working-through the past: it is a buried and stratified past, whose components are never lost and everything can virtually be brought back to light. Freud himself, however, added very different and more complex concepts to this rather static picture, such as: *Nachträglichkeit*, already surfacing in the *Studies on Hysteria*; the repeated translations of *Wahrnehmungszeichen*, to which he refers in the 112/1896 letter to Fliess; the bidirectionality of psychic processes that he introduces in the *Interpretation of Dreams*; the trend towards re-actualization of primary phantasies; the contradictory coexistence of an archaic time and a historicized time in the splitting that marks fetishism and, finally, the truth of the trauma that, built up in the present of the analytic session, can at last be experienced. These conceptualizations underline the shift from time to temporalization; as in the above-mentioned transcription and re-signification procedures, it is the subject that makes her/his appearance. As a result, the crucial process of self-historicization begins, which interprets events and facts in order to construct a history that is capable of defining and specifying the subject's individual existence. Out of these conceptualizations it is evident that the unconscious – though described as timeless, as a result of its ignoring the very idea of death and of its being marked by unchangeability and the permanence of desire – is, nevertheless, involved in the dynamic coming and going of primary processes, in the regressions that surface in dreams, symptoms and other unconscious formations and derivatives, and in repetitions aiming at obliterating time. According to Kaës (2015), unconscious time pervades psychic time – or more exactly the subjective experience of time – and strains against it.

The French translation of *nachträglich* into *après-coup* emphasizes the idea of a discontinuous psychic time, marked by blows and interrupted by latencies, with a forceful option for a bidirectionality of the time arrow (Laplanche, 2006): a lucky circumstance of a translation that grasps more than what is expressed in the original text, through interpreting and transforming the author's intentions.

This leads us to the definition of the human subject's time as a *shattered time* (Green, 2000), because it is interwoven with the unconscious: according to Green, it is a time that no longer has anything to do with the idea of an ordered succession that follows the tripartition of past–present–future. In Winnicott's vision, this kind of time is very close to the negative: when the mother's absence exceeds the ability of the infant to preserve her representation, 'the baby's capacity to use the symbol of the union ceases' (Winnicott, 1966, p. 431). As a result, the psychic functioning is deformed, mainly in relation to transitional and symbolization processes, and only what is negative will be considered real. The infant's ability to measure time is therefore ontologically linked both to her/his somatic urges and to her/his ability to produce and keep an image of the caring adult, with a sense of being one: relationality is, therefore, a key dimension in the development of subjective temporality.

The complexity of subjective temporality is conveyed by Green (2002) through the image of a *tree of time*: a system of interdependent relationships in which different meanings are conveyed by reticular relationships or a tree-like structure (rather than by sequential processes) that go beyond the categories of space and time. In the associative discourse of the analytic session, *retroactive reverberation* and *anticipatory annunciation* bring into being a multidirectional, arborescent temporality, characterized by a movement of associative irradiation: the discourse elements, as a result of unconscious activation, following a retroactive or anticipatory path, either resonate or join together. In this regard, Green emphasizes that Freud had already highlighted the diachronic heterogeneity of the psychic apparatus, due to structural differences of psychic agencies and manifold forms of inscription of the different temporalities' effects. As a result of the opposition between the subject's and the other's time, with the latter doubled into an inner other, rooted in the body, and an outer other, which marks individual and group relationships, time is fragmented and its components are under mutual tension. Among these categories we also find transgenerational time, which reaches across generations and concerns a negative transmission of de-signified elements.

The Z family

I get a number of calls from Mrs Z, marked by an anxious tone and a sense of urgency, in which I register a foreign accent. I propose a meeting with the parents and their twenty-two-year-old daughter. However, only Cristina and her father arrive at the appointment. With his hands full of the wrappers of the drugs she is on, he looks like a person who wants to hurry things along, and quickly summarizes his daughter's history in order to leave her alone with me as soon as possible. Cristina hardly ever looks at me, keeps her eyes down and speaks in a monotonous, lifeless voice. Mr Z points out that, after several failed therapeutic attempts, about six months ago he called a boyhood friend who is a psychiatrist and lives in his hometown: now he can finally see his daughter recovering.

Cristina tells me how she moved to a foreign country in order to attend its prestigious university and then started feeling bad up to the point of no longer being able to get out of bed, let alone leave her bedroom. The phases of her illness match her movements to and from her home country (which is her mother's) and her radical switches from one branch of study to another (e.g. from neuroscience to international relations). As a result, I feel confused and bewildered by this pressing space–time coming and going.

The term depression is used in relation with the mother, who began suffering from depression around Cristina's present age. There are deep gaps in the family history about this topic, as well as in Cristina's experience when she was a child: she kept seeing her mother leaving and being absent without understanding the reason, until her nanny, still working in the family, told her about her mother's attempted suicide. 'It never comes up in conversation.' Only recently did Mrs Z, after reading Cristina's suicidal thoughts in her own diary, mention it.

Due to Mrs Z's diplomatic career, the family history is segmented by repeated moves, every three or four years; since Mr Z runs a restaurant in his wife's country, he only lives with the family on and off, changing country every six months. After completing her secondary studies, first Cristina and then her younger sister moved to a renowned foreign college to engage in university studies. After a first very difficult and strenuous year, distinguished by a deep feeling of climatic and human coldness, Cristina managed to study for one more semester, although in a state of deep pain and loneliness. Then she asked her parents if she could return home but, in order to be heard, she had to tell them about her suicide attempts, even if, from what she says, they appeared doomed to fail. The relationship with her mother's depression is very close: thanks to a tranquilizer sent by her mother, Cristina slept twenty straight hours, until her sister called and warned the parents. When she started feeling bad, Cristina attended a course for telephone support for young people who attempted suicide, in order to understand what these people feel like. At this point, the family moved to Italy.

Cristina has lately written to her mother: 'I cannot recover if you do not cure yourself too'.

First family session

During the first family session (without the younger sister who is continuing her studies abroad), Cristina gradually changes her first meeting posture (head down, gaze never turned to the speaker) and becomes more and more animated, particularly when addressing her parents. Mrs Z introduces herself stating she is happy to be here. She adds that Cristina is taking an effective treatment and is again the daughter they know, clever, mature...

Cristina: ...responsible...
Maria: perhaps it was the anxiety of not knowing what career to choose...
Cristina: That's not the reason!
M: Maybe it was me and my mother having the same problem...
Analyst: ...your mother?

C:	We lost her five years ago. She was a cheerful, participating person: she came over to our place for periods of two or three months...
M:	Cristina is learning Italian fast. Many people take a year off...
Analyst:	The family gathered together, now. All that is missing is Cristina's sister.
Enrico:	I've always lived like that, a few months away and then a few months at home. However, I was always very present and attentive to all of them. The only problem is this (pointing to Cristina), it was a bolt out of the blue! She was attending the university she had always dreamed of: when she was admitted she was incredibly happy. Then, I had to recall her... later on we tried again... Eventually I found this psychiatrist, a childhood friend of mine, and she is cheerful again, and enjoys meeting other people. Now she must understand what she wants to do, where to go... everyday she comes up with something new...
C:	I may not do everything I say, I am twenty-two!
E:	We are absolutely willing for her to do whatever she likes, she is good at everything... but it is for her... Cristina believes we too need to be cured: if you think so, we will.

 I remark that there is a side of presence, which is positive and happy; and a side of absence, which escapes understanding.

E:	Perhaps I should have paid more attention to Cristina's panic attack, when she was seven or eight, in Colombia. I thought she might need some help, but then I saw her doing well...
M:	We were in the US, Cristina was four, Agata two: a perfect life, a wonderful school! But then we had to move to Colombia, and the first year I was very depressed: I did not understand the language, the nanny had stayed in the US... After a while, however, we were fine, happy, and he was with me all the time. The two sisters get along well, Agata admires Cristina so much!

 I ask about this nanny, whether she had been a major figure in the family.

C:	She was not important to me. She came after a significant one, and then disappeared.
M:	The previous one was too hard, so my mother sent us a seventeen-year-old girl. She was young and wanted to study. It ended when she was seen carrying all her stuff away in a supermarket trolley.
C:	She told me she would leave.
M:	I was desperate, I had to leave for Colombia.

C: I comforted you. She asked me: 'If I leave, will you still be my friend?' It helped me.
M: People often want to stay in the US. Now she is happy; she got married.
C: I remember the worst part of Colombia, I could not understand, I felt that at home there was much distress.
M: I don't like to remember: everything was horrible for me, the school, the house, people... I don't want to remember bad things. I wished I could leave, then we moved to a new home. Later on, a lady came to work for us, Anna, who is still with us.

I ask about Cristina's 'panic attack'.

C: Before Colombia.
E: No, we were already there, it happened during a weekend, when we went to the falls. Then it waned...
C: A one-time thing.

I attempt to draw their attention to this inclination to isolate negative affects and experiences, and ask whether they tried to find an explanation. The falls might represent the experience of suddenly and uncontrollably plummeting, with an abrupt discontinuation of the smooth and predictable flow of life.

E: I can't think of a reason. The only thing is that it might run in the family (he is referring to his wife's and her mother's depression).
C: But didn't you think of anything?
E: I talked about it with your mother at the time: we thought about getting you some therapy, but you were so well again so quickly...
M: I think it was related to me.
C: Why didn't you do anything then?
E: Because you were such a happy girl... We weren't being superficial!
C: Why didn't you think about doing anything to prevent it?
E: Your mother was in treatment twice, first when I met her and then in Colombia.
C: Precisely!
E: Are you blaming me...?

I point out that it is not about blaming, but it appears to be the family's way: keeping out everything that hurts, only focusing on positive aspects.

M: It is related to me: I have always been a very happy mother, everything was perfect. When I talked to teachers, I was almost

	ashamed in front of the other mothers, because they told me that everything worked perfectly with my daughters. Cristina only had one difficult period: her age, university…
E:	In Colombia I was very close to my wife.
C:	As a child, I forgot all this, but later on when I was at university it was like going back to that time.
M:	She was so happy, she wished to attend international schools, she has always attended English language classes. But when she was there, she was doing too many things: she worked in the library, in the morning she prepared sandwiches…
C:	It's different for me, I do want to understand what happened.

I emphasize the importance of Cristina's effort to differentiate her feelings from her parents'.

Cristina nods, then unexpectedly states, referring to her father: 'He is a physician'.

E:	Yes, a dentist. I used to work in Turin, but at some point I realized that an era was over. So I moved to * (Mrs Z's country of origin) and started over: I met her there…
M:	The name Cristina is a homage to his mother whom I never met. I lived with my grandma, who had Italian origins and spoke the Venetian dialect.
C:	I am told that one day I'll get to be the Cristina I always was. Daddy, what do you think it means?
E:	Over the past two years I've been seeing you… I'm so tired of seeing you so sad, disconnected from life.
C:	I don't do it on purpose.
E:	I know, but I would like to get my daughter back!
C:	Yes, I know, but you always say: 'Come on, smile!' It's a great pressure!
E:	I shouldn't say it. But we aren't perfect. Having a suffering child, I think, is the worst pain ever. It was easier with my wife. Anyway, it's over: your smile is the best medicine!
C:	But I'm not your therapist! I can't bear such responsibility… It's the first time we can talk about this kind of things…
M:	I always thought we would settle in Italy one day, and we would speak Italian! Cristina is an artist!
E:	She can sing, play the ukulele and the guitar, she's great at drawing…

Cristina (says something to her mother in their language): If we never talk about difficulties, then it becomes harder and harder.

E: Do you think that?

I emphasize that two levels of experience are surfacing: on the one hand, the perfect, happy family and, on the other, the dark side of the family. These two levels were never to meet each other, resulting in stunted family growth.

C: I can't see why these are bad things, it's a challenge to face.

We discuss how to proceed. While Mr and Mrs Z express their concern about taking away room from Cristina, I propose to get together again. The younger daughter is soon arriving in Italy and will be able to join us in the sessions.

C: I feel much better, this is what I wanted! When I came back home, I would have liked to have a family meeting, but then I thought it would be hard to begin, or I would have talked without ever stopping...

Mrs Z nods.

E: If that's okay with you, it's okay for me too.

Temporality in the family

Time is a category in the human mind that is inextricably linked to the idea of death, although, for this very reason, it is never fully definable. Space and time are two structural and connotative elements of the family group: the family occupies the specific space of the home, together with the whole of its physical and metaphorical meanings that are also connected to the social environment, while each family member, throughout their life, occupies a different, specific place with a transformation of positions and distances among themselves. The other basic family organizer is time, which ties it to the history of its ancestors, from which the particular history of the family begins and is then projected into the future of descendants, in terms of narrations, expectations, assigned tasks, rites, myths, destinies and innovations. Specifically, time is personified by ties of kinship, which point out the time flow and show the direction of the exchanges of nourishment, affection, education, authority, identification and so on.

Human temporality, which Laplanche (1989) unravels both from cosmological time and the living organism time, cannot but involve subjectivity, in a movement of active temporalization by a human being who proves to be able to produce or create his/her own time, though always with the other's contribution. To this effect, the family is a key structure for processing alterity and continuity, both basic needs and essential challenges for all humans. Each new existence unfolds at the intersection point of otherness and alterity on the one hand, and the human narcissistic need for identity and continuity on the other. The family is the main tool for both working out and developing the opposition and entwining of continuity and alterity: the generation of new lives entails a 'reproduction' of past into future, but is also rooted in alterity, starting from the biological process of meiosis, in which a significant exchange of genetic material occurs that originates the most unpredictable features in the involved individuals. This component of absolute novelty might be viewed as the first hint at thirdness, dating from conception.

Kaës (2015) introduced the concept of intersubjective temporality with the aim of stressing that the rhythm of discontinuities and separations in the experience with the object, as well as inter-rhythmicity in its synchronic, heterochronic or dyschronic forms, contributes to the process of building temporality, historicization and subjectivation. If, according to Kaës, group time supports and transforms the individual time of the subject, then temporality acquires notably complex and stratified forms in the family, a group with a history in which a time-defined origin and end are lacking.

Hurry, difficulty in waiting, urgent requests are the first elements introduced by the Z family. The emergent time is that of Cristina's sickness, the rough chronology of her falling ill, which is always linked to the whole family's or its members' significant geographical shifts. It is also the time of the failed treatments or the long-awaited recovery, which seems to exempt the parents from a more substantial involvement in their daughter's cure. Even the account given shortly afterwards by Cristina is more detailed but still confused, hard to follow, with each element replaced by another one: places, people, activities, field of study… Her depression is one with her mother's.

The rhythm of the family history is articulated in a most complicated way, and closely intertwined with the space dimension: it is punctuated by the house moves due to the mother's work, with the background of the father's alternation of presence and absence, and by the daughters' departures towards foreign universities, located at distant latitudes, in environments in which mentality and lifestyle are deeply divergent from this family's traditions. These moves are marked out by factuality, which is never associated with a communion of expectations, motivations, nostalgias, regrets. Both in Cristina's and in her parents' accounts, at some point you find yourself in another continent, and there a new life begins that may be more or less happy: are we in the presence of an eternal rebirth, bound to confirm the individual's and family happiness and allowing the family members to leave behind them the spectre of depression?

From the very first session, indeed, the mother's depression, rooted in the grandmother's, appears in Cristina's account as the gap, the disruption of the intertwined rhythms that make up the frame of family life, and what cannot either be said or thought. Cristina's attempted suicide, followed by her wish to volunteer in a listening centre for young people who have attempted desperate acts, looks closely related to Mrs Z's severe depressive crisis when Cristina was a little girl. With regard to these events the gaps become more clear-cut, the silence more absolute, and the girl's inability to understand more complete and annihilating. In this way Cristina expresses her need, her dire necessity to talk and understand, almost re-actualizing in *après-coup* what was once perceived but not comprehended, giving way to a terror attack in her as a child: in turn an inexplicable and isolated episode within a general attitude of happiness. The nanny alone, who is a steady presence within the family, broke that unsustainable silence, assuming the family function of an element of continuity and giving words to what was happening, naming what the others never acknowledged. The time obliteration that characterizes depression, due to a cessation of mourning processes and psychic work, here extends through the generations, becoming implacably actual in the daughter's/granddaughters' lives. Nevertheless, Cristina, who has already experienced short psychotherapy attempts, interrupted by her moves, appears to believe in the importance of broadening the questions raised by the individual members' psychic pain to the family space and to the time of the history of past generations. Moreover, Cristina has been carrying out the function of co-therapist since the beginning of our therapeutic relationship, daring to prompt unanswered questions and involving her father and, above all, her mother in a family request for treatment: 'I cannot recover if you do not cure yourself too'.

And yet the denial is absolute, impervious at the beginning: the depressed daughter is disavowed, ignored, rejected. The 'true' Cristina is the clever, mature, responsible girl, possibly in difficulty for the choice of a study path. Depression can only be a genetic issue, and the depressed grandmother is described as a cheerful and participating member of the family... Cristina's illness has consequently been *a bolt out of the blue*! Here is the trauma that keeps happening without warning, unrepresentable, unnameable, through a repetition that nullifies time and memory: the urgency of the opening demand becomes thereby understandable, with its aim to erase the painful experiences that require no less than an absolute rejection of time. The disorganizing event is located outside both temporality and subjectivity. A time (and a subject) for elaboration and transformation or overcoming, as is the case in the work of mourning, is neither available nor conceivable. On the contrary, (im-)personal actualization rules and forces everything to be instantly consumed, without any transformation, waiting for the recurrence of the 'same'. Green proposes the term *amnesic memory* to refer to the repetition coaction way of working, out of memory, within an absolute positivity that leaves no room for the work of the negative (repression, negation…). We are confronted not only with an *en bloc* mobilization but also with a subtly constructed, implacable mechanism, which can rule in minute detail the course of a destiny (Green, 2002). The family perspective gives us an idea of the effractive power of trauma: it is not limited to a tearing up of individual psychic boundaries, but violently and massively spreads to the family boundaries and broadens both spatially to multiple family members and temporally throughout generations.

While Mr Z is looking for explanations and solutions in tangible and factual elements, such as his daughter's difficulty in the choice of a study course, short glimpses are offered about the mother's depression, which Maria immediately shuts out through a cover of happiness. At the same time, Cristina's role of taking up the weight of breaks and lacerations becomes clear, as well represented in the incident of the disappeared nanny. If time is annihilated, the same goes for causal relationships, which are its consequences, and could have mitigated what otherwise recurs as unpredictable and alien (*uncanny*), because it escapes the reassuring cause–effect relationship. Memory, with its linking function of different and distant temporal elements, is firmly refused if it deals with painful experiences: these then have to be re-presentified in the daughters' lives. The two girls are also faced with radical changes in places and ways of life that in turn reactivate past experiences ('as a child, I forgot all this, but when I was at university it was like going back to that time'. 'I do want to understand what happened'). Family time, between recollection and repetition, engages and binds all members in a complex entwining of motions with multiple directions.

One more radical break occurs in Mr Z's life. He drastically left behind all previous relationships and achievements, generalizing his own experience as the 'end of an age'. In his account, a self-generative phantasy appears, while his wife steps in to emphasize his indissoluble bond with the mother object, even more relevant since it is lost for him and absent for her, who replaces it with her mother's mother, as a bearer of the origins issue. Once again, it is Cristina who embodies this bond. The block of time hints at death, which often appears in different moments and characters of the present and past family history, blaming the primary object inadequacy: the primary object, indeed, through its swinging between presence and absence and the periodicity of its investment, is the main organizer of temporality, provided that the wait and the need to delay are not expanded beyond the subject's ability to tolerate them.

Cristina questions her father about her own identity, thus expressing an acute identity anxiety she begins to be able to formulate: she also points out the inadequacy of her efforts to conform to her father's expectations and complains of pressure in this respect, up to the urge to become her father's therapist. Thus she manages to make a stand against her parents' repeated efforts to underline the relationship between the family's perfect happiness and her prospect of life and creativity, leaving aside the negative elements. My proposal to proceed through a family setting appears to offer Cristina not only a place for talking, questioning her parents and asking for information and explanations but also a temporal organization that allows her to overcome the difficulty in beginning to talk or in stopping, and to discover an expressible form for her and the whole family's experiences. It is almost as though the synchronic and diachronic dimensions of the family setting are the only ones that allow entry to a world closely intertwined with time and marked by its rhythm, discontinuity and affective interpunction (Green, 2002).

Space and time working-through by the Z family

In the first family session, the second-born's absence is clearly perceived: Agata appears to be kept safe, far from any problem, in contrast to her sister who is a threat to the picture of a happy, agreeable family, with all members concurring to the success and perfection of the whole. But even in the following session vague references are made to a time of crisis that Mrs Z minimizes, ascribing it to Agata's comparing herself with her boyfriend, who is a competitive and successful American, and charging her husband for dramatizing what she considers only a 'normal, natural' difficulty. Time returns at the opening of the second session, in a contrast between the 'Italian' idea of punctuality and that of the mother's country, resulting in Mr Z accusing her and Cristina of being always late. Delay is experienced by Mr Z as an irreparable absence, a painful expulsion from the other's mind. Cristina goes on trying to connect her problem with the family history and with their mutual links, while her father acknowledges, with intense grief and emotion, that he never coped with changes and pain through a shared dialogue. Cristina's anguished question reappears: 'But who is the Cristina I always was?' It appears to be a stronger and stronger complaint against the tendency to dissolve an articulated temporality into a mythical and undifferentiated time.

In the following sessions Cristina is increasingly lively and dynamic, and carries out her role of being the driving force of the family work, switching between an explosive mode and protective attitudes particularly towards her father, while often excluding her mother. Cristina becomes the spokesperson for the unrecognized and concealed family anxieties, daring to name the latent and shared family fear of actually being a 'failing family'. Her associations give form to her old feelings of emptiness, of lacking a foundation to lean on, which she shares with her sister. Her mention of not being able to tolerate the winter cold in the university town, as well as the summer heat in the Mediterranean country where her parents would have liked to organize a holiday at the onset of her psychic breakdown, expresses her feeling of being exposed, defenceless, deprived of a protective screen. At this juncture Mr Z recalls a question asked by his daughters, then in their teens, that really struck him: 'So, do we have a home?' Only then did he feel the responsibility of never having offered his family a place where they could imagine and locate themselves, and then devoted himself to buying and restructuring a house that he finally showed to his daughters as 'our home'. But it was too late, and this home never became more important than the uncles', cousins' and grandmother's houses, where their belongings scattered and got lost during holidays.

Agata, too, attends the fifth family session, having just arrived from the foreign country in which she attends university: she looks extremely worn out, fragile and flimsy, much more so than I had expected on the basis of her parents' accounts, with a distinctly depressive habitus. She proves anyway to be very involved in the session topics and course, and shows a transference that associates her sister and me as sources of differentiating thought, opposed to the parents' view of a blended and confused family.

But later on, though Cristina persists with her request to continue the family work, I find myself up against unannounced setting changes: at one session Cristina comes alone; at others Agata or Mr Z are absent… These changes are ascribed both to fortuitous circumstances and to the presumed need that therapeutic work should be focused on Cristina, about whom the first request was made.

The regular rhythm of sessions is now and then modified by the scheduling of family trips; likewise, the arrival of Agata's boyfriend upsets the family's time and space organization. During his visit, he sleeps in Cristina's room, while Mrs Z, worried about possible desperate acts by Agata, takes her younger daughter into her own bed. The recrudescence of death anxieties and suicidal phantasies, together with the role that the family bestows on the young American man of an unsettling and threatening alterity, pushes the family to merge into a state of undifferentiated, archaic unity.

In a following session, Cristina thanks everybody for coming, stressing how 'we all speak more openly now; these are difficult but significant discourses'. However, the more Cristina feels better, being able to articulate both her own individual and the family group discourse, the more Agata's suffering becomes acute and desperate: she rejects the psychiatrist's diagnosis of depression, blaming herself for her condition, due to laziness, ineptitude and being wrong. She specifically points to the future breaking in to her life as the cause of her sickness. 'Once I used to see only good things': her inability to yield to psychic work – mourning, the negative – forces her to resume the phantasy of a return to the womb and to the idea of being bound to stay for ever with the parents. Time is now the threatening object against which to protect oneself: 'I cannot get ready in time'.

In this painful session, after Mrs Z stated one more time the myth of the family perfection, Cristina bitterly remarks she never had an identity card, but only copies of it, and summarizes her parents' attitude towards their daughters:

> You need not worry
>
> You have to be responsible
>
> You need not think.

The parents only seem capable of expressing their bewilderment, returning to the subject of a lacking primary environment that can ensure survival. Mrs Z: 'I bought vegetable roots to make Agata and Cristina put on weight...but we don't have roots!' Mr Z: 'I'm a fish out of water... moreover I'm deaf.'

After a cancelled session for the family vacation in a Mediterranean country, the father comes with his wife and daughters to the next session, but remains outside, entrusting them with the task of embodying the family and transgenerational depression as a purely feminine matter. Feelings of irreparable rupture transpire through a surface attitude of lightness and relaxation: news about losses reached them while on vacation; Agata was left by her boyfriend and, in turn, stopped the Skype sessions she had begun with a therapist who could speak her mother tongue.

Concluding reflections and working hypotheses

The Z family appears to be haunted by a shared phantasy of the immobilization of time as the only defence against a recurrence of anxiety and pain. Separations, losses and anguishes of abandonment by the object are at the origin of revivals and actualizations that result in temporal gaps that need to be closed as soon as possible: the individual members' suffering cannot therefore be hosted and thought by the others, but only put away into a limbo of obscurity and incompatibility, while expecting everything to return to how it always used to be and the perfect family picture to be unfailingly reconstructed once more. On encountering this family, I perceive a scattering into a form of pre-subject temporality similar to what Kaës (2015) named *group achrony*, an archaic configuration marked by the absence of boundaries and the confluence of psychic spaces, resulting in affects and representations indiscriminately pertaining to all family members. It may be considered a time without temporality, caught between the promise of erasing history, namely castration and death (*ucrony*), aiming at leaving room for an absolute and perfect happiness, and the time of annihilating disaster and suffering. In order to save the unity and cohesion of the family group, individual temporalities are stifled or annihilated in the bud, thus nullifying the threat of disintegration resulting from the geographical distancing of family members and blocking the daughters' individuation processes.

A more dynamic, conflicting temporality makes its appearance within the predefined and protected boundary of the sessions: only there, perhaps, the link with the other that opens to a subjective time or transitional time (Green, 2002) becomes possible. The accounts of individual histories, so far confined to unreachable psychic areas, come to light and are integrated anew into a history of the family group, in which continuity, repetitions and revival can be identified along with discontinuities, conflicts and sinking: as a result, areas of shared experience and the resumption of subjectivation processes become feasible. Using Kaës's conceptualizations again, the onset of a symbolic time entails the articulation of a singular subjectivity with the group temporality, without the risk of killing oneself or the family group, and the production of a dyschrony within the group that overlaps with the *ability to be alone in the group*. The subject's temporality, rooted in the somato-psychic relationship with the primary object and in the transmission processes between generations, expands and complexifies within the specific group that is the family, implicated in turn in a ceaseless spatio-temporal motion to which members and links among them contribute. The family group temporality therefore appears to be made up of the time of the succession of generations and of the flow of unconscious legacies to children and grandchildren, along with the intersection of individual and group temporalities. The result is an undecidable region of temporality, where relations among different times become more significant than the times themselves, similarly to what happens, in a spatial dimension, with the construction of intersubjective links: might it be, then, an interpenetration of links and temporality?

The extension both in space and time of the psychoanalytic method, replacing the archaeological model with a transformative one (Botella, 2014), enables us to grasp more thoroughly the psychic way of working of people who consult us, inasmuch as they share links that are articulated in space as well as in time, both in an intersubjective and group dimension.

> Everyone always says it's good to have roots. I'm convinced that the only creatures who really do have roots – trees – would prefer not to have any: then they'd be able to get on an aeroplane.
>
> Bertold Brecht (1961)

Chapter 6

Musical dialogues: The baby in a world of sound and rhythm

> When mothers have children suffering from sleeplessness, and want to lull them to rest, the treatment they apply is to give them, not quiet, but motion, for they rock them constantly in their arms; and instead of silence, they use a kind of crooning noise; and thus they literally cast a spell upon the children ... by employing the combined movements of dance and song as a remedy.
>
> Plato (*Laws*, VII, 790d–790e)

When does the dialogue between parents and baby begin? Winnicott highlighted the mirroring function of the mother's gaze in the birth of self, while Lacan conferred a key role to the mirror stage in the Ego building. We know that in Western culture the *gaze*, or the dialogue among gazes, is viewed as central in interpersonal relationships, mainly at the birth of the mother–infant relationship, and its disorders are considered a specific sign of suffering in the relationship of the baby with caring adults and with the world in general. Ajuriaguerra (1959) introduced the concept of *tonic dialogue*, a form of bodily discourse that can be observed when a parent holds her/his baby and works through a dynamic mutuality of posture and adaptation. It is a form of primary communication in which, through changes in muscular tone, making faces, overall motions and even rests, the infant reacts to external and internal stimuli, while her/his mother as well, through her whole body, interprets, understands and answers: the parent–infant dyad is thus laying the foundations of their own style of relationship, grounded on mutuality, which entails both continuity and discontinuity. Anzieu (1979), in turn, starting from the *sound bath* the infant is immersed in, and from the sound envelope that contains mother and baby, making them a one, described the existence of a *sound mirror* and an audio–phonic skin at the beginning of life: they participate in building the self as a psychic pre-individual whole and lay the foundations of the processes of becoming able to signify and symbolize, well before the emergence of the phenomena of visual mirroring described by Lacan and Winnicott.

Conversely, the *sound dialogue* originates long before, at least in the fifth month of gestation, when the hearing apparatus is already working, allowing the first sound and rhythmic experiences and memories that spring from the interweaving of movements by the mother's and foetus's bodies with the sounds produced by the mother's body and voice organs, as well as by the external world. It is, therefore, not only the newborn but the foetus too, who lives immersed in a sound bath that becomes more and more well-defined and recognizable. Before the sense of hearing has become fully operational, the foetus perceives sounds as vibrations, tactile and motion sensations, that are filtered for it by the amniotic fluid and are often associated to the mother's body's internal movements, shifts and swinging in space: the foetus's primary relationships with the mother and, through her, with the world, is a musical relationship. As Fornari wrote: 'In the beginning was the sound, the sound was with the mother, and the sound was the mother' (1984, author's translation). The sound envelopes the foetus, which becomes an integral part of it, through its own movements and shifts.

Suzanne Maiello (1993, 2013) used the term *sonorous object* 'to describe the ensemble of the prenatal reminiscences, sonorous and rhythmic quality that the child keeps in his memory after birth', including the mother's voice (2013, p. 26). The sound of the mother's utterances is characterized by qualitative constancy and temporal discontinuity and has the function of introducing the *difference principle* already in prenatal life. The early forms of representation might therefore be sonorous in nature and precede visual ones. Infant research studies have proved that the newborn identifies her/his mother's voice before her face, but even during pregnancy parents may note specific reactions by the foetus towards one or the other of the parents' voices. Discrimination is helped by the several senses implied in the perception of musical elements and the human voice: in addition to hearing, vibratory, proprioceptive and tactile sensorialities are especially activated in the restricted uterine environment. The experience of listening to oneself while producing sounds, as well as the proprioceptive perception of one's own movements and body positions in space, by far precedes self-awareness as the other's visual object, in mirroring phenomenon.

Psychic activity descends from these very pre- and perinatal experiences, whose richness allows them to be defined as musical in all respects: in the previous chapters, I have dealt extensively with the sharing of formal qualities by music and the psyche, such as the tension between expectation and resolution, crescendo and diminuendo, consonance and dissonance, as well as essential modes of working, such as the work of mourning, of the negative, of nostalgia,[1] all centred on the temporal element. It is the intersubjective origin of the psyche, which begins with the encounter with the affective and musical other, including the other of one's own body (Aulagnier, 1975).

Neuroscientists have recently detected, particularly in musicians, the presence of specific, audiovisual mirror neurons that can coordinate and interpret connections between motion and sound and that are essential for choosing and producing sounds. Such a system reflects the close interdependence since the earliest stages of the human subject's psychomotor organization between the different forms of sensoriality and motor-gestural organization that take part in sound, rhythm and music perception and production. With respect specifically to sound perception and decoding, neuroimaging studies have pointed out specific hemispheric areas in the newborn brain that can interpret structured sets of sounds, favouring rhythms that match those of bodily processes. In accordance with the discovery by language evolution students that musical language is acquired before verbal and gestural expressions (Brandt, 2009), we are faced by a neural organization that is originally appointed to elaborate musical syntax and, with just a slight reorganization, becomes capable of supporting also language perception and production (Turner and Ioannides, 2009). The greater bilateral distribution of cerebral areas destined to music rather than to language, and the inborn ability to be affected by music lead to the consideration that language is a highly specialized subclass of musical cognition.

Music allows a vivid experience of affects, though without defining their object and content, precisely because form and content lose their differentiation and verge on overlapping: something similar to what Ogden (1989a) names *the primitive edge of experience*, in which surfaces and epidermal sensations are the basis for self-experience, and there is neither inside and outside, nor self and other. Sensory experience is the infant itself, and all discontinuities of form, symmetry, rhythm, skin pressure and so on make the baby feel completely inexistent. The same is true for musical experience, which is made of dynamic movements of presence/absence and continuity/discontinuity. According to Ogden, this way of working marks all the stages and moments of psychic life, in which the *autistic–contiguous* organization works as a foundation and background for all other modes of organizing experience. Though Ogden does not mention a sound envelope like Anzieu does, he emphasizes the simultaneous working of the three positions among which the paranoid–schizoid position induces rupture, splitting and fragmentation, which are required to allow movement and the creation of original structures.

The sound environment at the origins of life

Music, as the earliest kind of language from both an ontological and a phylogenetical view, is to be considered the primal language, a proper *Ursprache* that, since the earliest stages of life, affects the original impact with the world and psychic experience up to *musical weaning*, when the word appears (Lecourt, 2011). Auditory experiences are the original link between the concreteness of somatic experience (which is also psychic, simply because it is experience) and the abstraction of psychic activity that works mainly through visual images (Ciccone et al., 2007). Based on the assumption of the intersubjective origin of the unconscious, which springs from the fundamental anthropological situation of a newborn that is nurtured by an adult (Laplanche), it is possible to hypothesize, since intrauterine life, a sensorial pre-unconscious, whose musical component produces the first traces of discontinuity and rhythm: in addition to these, the perception of the mother's and the foetus's bodily motions begins to prepare, through a sense of difference and change, the experience of space and time. These early traces too, like the sexual unconscious, are inextricably dependent on the other, who is originally perceivable through the unpredictable and uncontrollable changes that the primordial being endures, what Gaddini (1969) called *to imitate in order to perceive* and *to imitate in order to be*.

We must be aware, anyway, that the newborn is no longer just a listener, but produces sounds that she/he, as well the environment, can perceive, in their dynamic inner–outer interdependence: in addition to crying, which heralds her/his coming into the world, many other sounds made by her/his own body outline a sound space that, starting from a first space–auditory image, predicts the creation of a psychic space.

In *Project for a Scientific Psychology* (1895), Freud pointed out the association between the newborn's scream and the other's (*nebenmensch*) specific act as the activator of the secondary function of understanding and being understood, leading to the outlining of a boundary between self and not-self, the infant's first step towards becoming a subject. A. S. Cismaresco (1993), in turn, described the newborn's crying as an *acoustic umbilical cord* due to its facilitating role in the newborn's transition from prenatal life to future autonomy. It arouses movements within the family group, furthering closeness between parents and baby. The newborn's absolute helplessness is so reduced by the attraction and call power of her/his scream, which endows her/him with a soloist role (Lecourt, 1994). The newborn begins to appropriate the sound space precisely through her/his scream, as it spreads throughout the external, as well as the internal, space. At the beginning, indeed, sounds spread throughout the environment, and the sound experience is marked by a lack of limits, of reference points and of organization. Boundaries will gradually be drawn later, during the interactions with the external world, following effects and reactions from the environment, leading to experiences of intrusion and leakage. As to the temporal dimensions, sounds appear to have acquired a more definite structure already in intrauterine life, when the mother's bodily sounds and voice, embedded in feelings of motion, already offered the foetus an experience of discontinuity and difference.

In order for the newborn to acquire the ability to perceive a sound envelope as a primitive sketch of a boundary that is not only individual but also pluri-subjective and bidirectional, with both an outward and an inward side, a remarkable psychic work is required to organize and structure the sound experience: this psychic work needs the support offered by the holding and the reverie function of the nurturing environment, which elaborates and psychifies the sound, and is endorsed, in turn, by the larger, social environment that provides specific cultural forms and sound relations. The differentiation between noise and music, related with aggression and love, which will be present at some point, appears to be the first sign of sound discrimination, matching paranoid–schizoid processes. According to Lecourt (2006), this music/noise splitting provides a function of *demarcation signifier* (Rosolato, 1985), namely of limiting, outlining and opposing.

The family receives the newborn, and earlier the foetus, into a sort of familial soundtrack that is a specific expression of the family group's psychic structure. Édith Lecourt names this family music *bruissement familiale*, or familial rustling: it supports the creation of a psychic sound–musical envelope that contains and protects, but mainly communicates and allows differentiation between internal and external spaces. On the one hand, there is the internal perception by the newborn of its own scream, of its echoing in the acoustic space and the reception and answer that is received; on the other, the expecting and welcoming world is characterized by heterophony and heterorhythmicity, namely by the compresence of voices with different and often dissonant pitches, timbre, intonation, rhythm and melodic profiles. Lecourt (2011) describes the group dimension of the family sound world with the expression *family vocal group*, namely, the orchestration of sound and music within the family: 'The sound set of the family environment (voices/noises/music) in which the foetus is bathed during gestation, and which the newborn discovers in the form of a chorus of satisfaction/pleasure (choir of muses) or depression/violence (the Furies), already in the good/bad split' (ibid., p. 122, author's translation). It is the place where the first acoustic impressions are formed that will be reference points for the subject's future discriminations, propensities and productions.

Albeit through the sound deformations caused by the watery uterine environment, the foetus begins to familiarize with this world of sounds, whose impression will affect the duration, intensity and modulations of the baby's crying at birth (Lecourt, 1994). The family sound group also has the function of metabolizing external environment sounds and noises, allowing the baby to develop, between inside and outside, her/his own sound identity: the heterophony of the family vocal group lays the foundations of polyphony and harmony within the weave of plurisubjective links, though when brought to the extremes either of absolute heterophony and chaos or of homophony and unison it can result in severe deformations of sound identity or sound spaces. The babblings whereby the baby debuts on the family stage are therefore the end product of a musical world made up of plural relationships that channel them into a polyphonic discourse, which is composed of an interweaving of the horizontal/spatial motion of individual voices with the vertical/concurrent meeting of sounds: this is exactly what makes the difference between musical and verbal discourses, the latter requiring, in order to be understandable, that voices alternate on a single horizontal plane.

The subject's identity develops within this sound and rhythmic whole that characterizes each family vocal group: in the space between heterophony, possibly resulting in absolute confusion and loss of meaning, and homophony, which tends to cancel differences, a multi-vocal listening ability comes to light, mainly in adolescence, that allows the distinction and understanding of more than one voice in the same music.

Nursery rhymes, lullabies and babblings

Though rhythmic–phonic games are usually introduced to young children, particularly through nursery rhymes, they are a significant part of babies' own impetus to sound production. According to Fornari (1984), they have the function of 'restoring the original oneness by recovering original sounds and rhythms that, though speaking in this world, speak about another world' (ibid., p. 11, author's translation), and are part of transitional phenomena. The baby's pleasure in listening to and repeating nursery rhymes does not refer to the evident meaning of the words, but to 'a sort of primary sound' that is made up of pure rhythm and intonation, characterized by homophonia, and of rhyme specularity. Even the infant's earlier sucking activity used to have a rhythmic structure, shaped by the mother's heartbeat rhythm, which was anticipated, during intrauterine life, by the foetus's thumb sucking. The significant sound–rhythmical component of the primary experience of feeding outlines the inherent musicality of human intersubjectivity, enhanced by the infant's simultaneous dreaming state.[2] This appears to be one more form of specularity between pre- and post-natal experience, in which music plays a linking function that, leading back to what was already known, allows the exploration of what is new and the symbolic recovering of what was lost in the real. Phonic and musical playing, together with the involved somatic component of motion and tonic changes, as well as sensorial reflectivity, denotes for the infant an active reproduction of her/his own good experiences of holding and handling. It is far from being a solipsistic activity, since an inherent part of it is the elicitation of similar activities in the other.

Piaget (1947) already highlighted the role of repetition in cognitive development, between adaptation and accommodation processes, but I believe he neglected to draw attention to their affective and mainly musical components, which make them creative acts. In music, we have to add the intellectual pleasure of investing musical laws and the symbolic pleasure of subjective expression to the sensorimotor, auditive, vibratory, gestural and tactile pleasures. Here, the body plays less than a secondary role, being a whole with the music and, when there is one, with the musical instrument. Similarly, little Ernst (Freud, 1920) added sound repetition to his own gestural iteration: a repetition that changed according to the associated motion in space. In order to symbolically elaborate the experiences of separation and rejoining, the musical element is needed, more inclined than the action of playing to include and signify the affect, and also to further the introjection of a relationship due to its inherent linking structure. Repetition, which is an acted form of memory, is associated to the future event, opening the dimension of the present to subjective time. As a result, repetition escapes the deadly fate of repetition compulsion, teaming up with the lively drive part. As for the experience of separation and absence, it is part and parcel of music, which represents it by silence: as I already mentioned, according to Busoni the essence of music resides in the pause and *corona*, whereas Miles Davis stated that true music is silence while the notes merely frame it. Even in the adult–baby relationship pauses play a crucial role, as proved by infant research studies that highlight rhythmic specificity and mutuality in the interactive and sound exchanges between infant and caretakers.

Silence and pauses produce thinking and symbolization if they are underlain by a time of movement: the time of expectation and memory, a time that moves forwards and backwards building boundaries in eternity and mobilizing stillness and unchangeability. As a result, memory and expectation are imbued with time, but they also depend on the lively presence of the other, who has the role of proffering an answer to the infant's needs in a time that is sustainable for her/him. The construction of time is therefore based both on the infant's somatic urges and on her/his ability to produce and save the image of a caring and holding adult with whom she/he can experience her/himself as a whole, and at the same time perceive as the rescuing other.

Imitation, repetition and variation are distinctive features of *motherese*, the unique communicative style that mothers, and adults in general, implement when talking with newborns and babies, as well as of lullabies, nursery rhymes and sound games that the baby creates in her/his early vocalizations and subsequent babbling. Besides repetition and imitation, *motherese* is marked by high-pitched sounds, exaggeration of affective expressions and melodic contours, syntactic simplicity, segmentation and onomatopoeia. The slow and monotone rhythm may become accelerated, as in some kinds of rhymes and vocal games. Such specificity of rhythm, melody and prosody has a key role in the development of mutuality in the primary relationship, by activating the baby's social undertaking that in turn gives rise to and confirms the parental identity.

Many of these elements are shared by lullabies, though with lower registers and a more steady and uniform rhythm, which is based on the frequencies of physiological rhythms already experienced during intrauterine life, and therefore produces the desired hypnotic effect. In many cultural contexts, the singing addressed to newborns is often choral and has a pronounced ritual meaning, aimed at transmitting the idea of belonging and initiation in relation to the social and cultural world that is welcoming the newborn, with its values and laws. In Western countries, the lullaby often has the features of a traditional song with a simple and repetitive structure: yet it is strongly embedded in the original culture of which it expresses myths, histories and legends, as well as individual and group affective dynamics. It helps, thereby, to transmit the social group discourse that lies at the basis of the narcissistic contract stipulated by all subjects with the group they belong to. In addition, the key role of subjective interpretation and improvisation in the lullaby has the function of shaping musical and verbal contents according to the specific relationship between baby and caretaker. The singing joins with rocking movements, themselves characterized by rhythm and repetition, a proof of the deep link between sound and motion in the fusion of the mother's and infant's bodies. Memories of these sensory experiences connected to the sound of the voice can be found in linguistic expressions, such as those qualifying words and voices as warm, velvety, metallic, biting and so on. Variations of rhythm, intensity and tone reflect a constant mutual adjustment between the baby's and the adult's expressions, while the regulation of distance and direction of sound stimuli participate in the definition of subjective and intersubjective sound space.

All the musical forms that inform the primary relationship – often named as echo, mirror, rhyme, repetition – appear to be ruled by the sensation of a closed time, a predictable and soothing return of the same, as well as a space whose qualities of internal and external, same and other, me and not-me are not yet defined. Imberty (2002) states that, in this harmonious state, mother and baby may endlessly perform their separating and meeting again, since time remains closed and devoid of a proper unpredictable flow towards the future, which is projected towards death. Yet, since there is no perfect imitation or precise repetition, the other creeps in and opens this space and time, making these experiences lively and playful. Here is the absolute heterogeneity between the baby experiencing all this within a significant human relationship or being confronted with a repeated identical registration, unless integrated by the presence of a caretaker who interprets by adding meaning, affect and subjectivity to plain auditory, visual or any other perceptions. Even if it protects from separation, loss and mourning, this transitional time in which present, past and future are still inconceivable is, according to Imberty, an intermediate time between the archaic atemporality of self and the developing environment that will soon shape the Ego identity.

Music and the word

The word, too, is strongly rooted in its musical origins, which are expressed by its sound–musical component: moreover, the pronounced word needs to be articulated by voice organs, thus arousing specific proprioceptive perceptions of movement, vibration and contact that are added to the perception of the produced sound. The first sounds that the newborn articulates have a guttural quality, such as *gh*, *kh*. A few weeks later, they become *ghe*, *ke*, as a result of the concurrence of two opposite forces: the former expels the air from the lungs, the latter holds it back by means of the larynx. Not only do these sounds have a strong affective meaning but also the memory of them is enclosed in words that refer to muscularly demanding actions such as *to gulp, to gag, to growl, to cry, egoism, aggression, anxiety* and so on, revealing the original intention of grabbing and holding, namely of discriminating and asserting.

This complex sensory structure of the word that is pronounced, listened to or thought is responsible for its constant resonance with unconscious mnestic traces. According to Fédida (2012), it is the ununderstood sound fragment that feeds the phantasy, and the specificity of our psychoanalytical listening is addressed right to this meaningful emptiness. Freud repeatedly dealt with the opposition between hearing/intending and understanding that is involved in the source of phantasies: the infant, who cannot use words, listens to conversations that she/he therefore cannot understand until later, in the *après-coup*. 'The phantasies arise from things *heard* but only understood *later*, and all the material is of course genuine' (letter to Fliess of 2 May 1897: Freud, 1887–1902, no. 61, p. 196). This sound material expresses the extraneous at work in the most secret psychic areas, which the word transmits without us knowing, conveying an unknown content. It is, therefore, the phonic component of the interpreting words that, according to Fédida, returns to the patient a sound material marked by an uncanny, intimate strangeness and succeeds in touching the unconscious. If the analyst gives up this position of intimate stranger, his/her understanding remains confined to a conscious dimension of mere empathic understanding: a word will work as an interpretation only if it can re-echo the sensory kernel of the heard and de-signified word (Galiani, 2012). The word, in its corporeity and sensoriality, is therefore the carrier of experiences closest to the unconscious, so we should not be surprised when it is chosen as the preferential working tool in newborn psychoanalysis and psychotherapy, as powerfully demonstrated by Johan Norman's and Björn Salomonsson's work.

Music and transitional processes

Intersubjectivity is a key element in all stages through which the baby acknowledges, elaborates, memorizes and practises producing communicative sounds. Researchers detected that even in songbirds the neurons in the cerebral cortex attune to rhythmic and sound qualities of songs heard from adult specimens present in the environment, regardless of their belonging to the same species or supposed genetic determinants: the learned singing takes on the vocal characteristics of the song the juveniles were exposed to at the beginning of life (Moore and Woolley, 2019). It is a similar phenomenon to the impression left by exposition in the uterus to a specific language, whether it coincides or not with the language spoken in the subject's family environment.

Music should be viewed as a transitional process and function not only because it is an art form, but also because its structure is centred in the *in-between*: music is basically made up of intervals, both with regard to melodies and harmonies, and to rhythm (time organization), which is made of the mutual reference of on-beats and off-beats, sounds and silences and sequences of differences. Lecourt (2011) defines it as a plural mode of relationship, a groupal and polyphonic structure, which concurrently unfolds along a vertical axis (harmony, rhythm) and a horizontal one (melody), unlike the verbal structure, which is monodic, with only space for one voice at a time. Musical weaning can be precisely described as the vertical axis taking second place in favour of a focus upon the horizontal one, through a kind of desensitization towards the harmonic components of sounds. The multidirectionality of sound transmission, together with the sensory richness of musical phenomena, brings borders between me and not-me into play, blurring sharp definitions and implying the listening function in all its forms, from the more passive up to the positively active, and from the most abstract up to the most concrete. In this respect, Jean Cocteau (1918) warned us: 'Beware of music. Look out! Be on your guard, because alone of all the arts, music moves all around you' (ibid., p. 11).

This incompatibility with sharp borders and well-defined contents makes music a deeply transformative language and experience, since they are embedded in time and are syntonic with the work of mourning, which is nothing but psychic work.

If the mother–infant relationship is first and foremost a musical relationship, giving rise to the newborn's psychic life, playing with listening to the self and the other and with vocalizing and producing sounds are mainly transitional and plural phenomena. From these the subject's Ego can emerge as a signifying and symbolizing agent that can relate to reality and fantasy.

Notes

1 For the *work of nostalgia*, see Ludovica Grassi, 'Affetti in transito' in Rosso C. (ed.), *Identità polifonica al tempo della migrazione*, Rome: Alpes, pp. 25–57.
2 The newborn's EEG recording during feeding shows a REM-type cerebral activity, allowing the hypothesis that, albeit awake, the infant experiences an oneiric state.

Chapter 7

The musical unconscious in the family

> Wittgenstein stated that what we cannot speak about we must pass over in silence. I would like to suggest a suitable paraphrase for our case: the truth that we cannot speak about we must sing it, say it in music. With that, I'll bid you farewell.
> (With these words, Luciano Berio greeted his public in 2003, shortly before his death.)
> Luciano Berio (2006, p. 110, author's translation)

Everybody may happen to walk through a small village or a particularly quiet city district during the summer and to hear sounds and noises from homes through the open windows: it is the music of families, different and specific for each one, made of low (adult males), medium (women) and high-pitched (children) tones and voices, laughs, cries, singings, calls and screams, coughs and sneezes, and also squeaks, screeches, crackles, bangs, and furthermore the radio, TV, music sound systems and many more noises. Sometimes smells from clothes hanging up to dry, kitchen aromas, or vanishing visions through windows and front doors, or from balconies and terraces add to the sounds. This is the sensory register that, further extended to touch and taste, and enriched with other countless qualities, makes the first family environment a prime and irreplaceable reference point for all individuals, in which they find a totality of impressions and experiences to compare with those they encounter outside of it. The primary interweaving of sensory traces and memories, unique for each individual, will be a filter and a basis of comparison for all subsequent experiences and will affect gestures, inclinations, cathexes and sense of identity throughout life, as a persistence of the earliest form of psychic organization. Gaddini (1968) viewed sensoriality as the cornerstone of primal psychic activity, which he described as mental pre-symbolic activity and psychosensory functioning; subsequently in 1980 (Gaddini, 2002), he specified that the basic mental organization, activated by the turmoil produced by separation processes and the emergence of needs, has the main task of constructing the first mental image of the body–self: according to Gaddini, this attribution of psychic meaning to the body and its functioning coincides exactly with the individual's psychic birth.

Sensoriality implies an encounter with the other, including the other of one's own body (Aulagnier, 1975). Assigning centrality to the unconscious, psychoanalysis focuses on the other inside ourselves, which is unknown and alien, but also our most familiar possession. We can only meet it through a transference relationship, which reveals the inadequacy of mere introspection. The analytic setting, through its non-processual component, promotes activation of our senses when we are with our patients: the couch–chair position restricts contact and mutual gaze while bringing hearing and sound production to the forefront.

Listening is, indeed, the basic tool of psychoanalysis, whose origins hinged on verbal language, though Freud never excluded obtaining and investigating body language, which can also be observed by the gaze. Psychic activity was, therefore, centred on conscious and preconscious word representations, equipped with an acoustic root, and above all on unconscious thing-presentations, mainly made up of visual images.

Music and psychic life

Music has the remarkable property of encompassing all the conceivable range between the concrete and the abstract: it originates in the body, in its movements and its ability to produce vibrations in the most diverse materials, from air to different objects and the materials from which musical instruments are made, including vocal cords, up to the organs of acoustic sensoriality, which involve all body surfaces, where vibrations are perceived. Nevertheless, its language has been considered so abstract as to trespass on pure mathematical thinking, up to the point that Busoni emphasized its immateriality and incorporeity (*sounding air*), foredooming it to be the most refined reflection of nature. This is perhaps why music is suited to represent all kinds of affects, albeit without dealing with their content.

Music infects with emotions and moods, cancels boundaries between subjects and fills up all spaces with its vibrations, between trespassing and intruding. At the same time, it is located in the intersubjective and is the *in-between* itself, both with regard to melody, which is made up of intervals between sounds that follow one another in time, and to harmony, which originates from overlapping sounds and the resulting chords: silence, which separates sounds and their sequences, is the very essence of music. Rhythm, too, requires more than one sound in sequence, thus contributing to make music a 'mode of plural relationships' (Lecourt, 2011, p. 119, author's translation) and to build up a polyphonic discourse made of the intertwining of horizontal/spatial and vertical/simultaneous motions. This is the main difference from verbal discourse, which is understandable only when the individual voices alternate on a single horizontal level. According to Lecourt, the musical interval, namely the interval between two sounds, is to be viewed as a metaphor for all human relationships and the point of departure of musicotherapy as a work focused on relationship and listening.

The role of kinaesthetic and proprioceptive sensibility, in addition to hearing sense, in musical reception, allows us to imagine how early each subject's rhythmic, sound and musical experiences and memories through his/her *sound body* must be (Brault and Marty, 2018). Moreover, bidirectional and reflective features of such perceptive modalities are expressions of their primary intersubjective core. Sound identity originates in body experience, inside the relationship with the other: 'The subject's sound space lies at the interface between the body and the environment' (ibid., p. 321, author's translation).

In previous chapters, I extensively analysed the many coincidences and overlaps between musical and unconscious psychic ways of functioning, starting from the essence of music as the art of sounds in the movement of time and its core in imitation and repetition, as well as in the work of mourning and of the negative. Psychic work, and specifically the work of the negative, results in the removal of unsignifiable and irregular sound frequencies (the noise) from the whole spectrum of sounds, letting a musical meaning and the timbre, namely the specific, individual quality of sounds, take shape. Musical notes result from a cultural selection of meaningful sounds from the whole range of perceptible sounds for the human ear, from the lowest up to the highest. Music, therefore, consists in a negative, an absence, intervals separating the different sounds that compose musical phrases and, likewise, the closeness or distance between the sounds that make up the chords of harmony: these specific relationships among sounds create the musical basis that, when listening to music, we can take for granted but that are also the foundations of the musical sense that each individual musician conveys through a specific combination of sounds and rhythms.

Moreover, music unfolds through a work of linking and unlinking, which is the core of the dynamics between life and death drives, while developing through succeeding translations of former contents and forms. All these elements contribute to its coherent structure as well as to the creation of ever new achievements. Even when repetition is applied indefinitely, as in some recent musical styles, it is just for its transformative attitudes upon the experiencing listeners (Deleuze, 1968). Repetition and confusion that result from unlinking are, likewise, the identifying expressions of the most unconscious layers of psychic life. Nathalie Zaltzman (1979) poignantly outlined an *anarchic drive* as a vital, rebellious, separating and even creative component of the death drive, apt to allow survival in extreme individual and social conditions: it can overcome the excess of linking that results in obliteration of both alterity and the dialectic same–other that are essential for life. While music can be defined as a form of time organization, possibly with a role in the genesis of temporality itself, time is a key component of psychic work too, such as in the work of mourning and of nostalgia, drawn out between de-cathexis and preservation. Difference and alterity, introduced in psychic life through imitation at the stage of overcoming fusionality and omnipotence, are represented in music by the other voice, either consonant or dissonant.

At different levels music can be considered also affected by the unconscious atemporality and by the bidirectionality of psychic processes: on first listening, we hear an ongoing development, but rhythm, silences and modulations impress discontinuity, while understanding and interpreting sounds *après-coup* is what makes up the musical discourse. Rather than a linear development, music listening and experiencing requires an uninterrupted coming and going, because each sound, rhythm or any other musical element gains sense and is transformed by everything that precedes or follows. Musical rhythm may even lose all its regular predictability and take on an asymmetric temporal structure, as is the case in some motion shapes that could be described as primeval, such as pelvic muscle movements during sexual intercourse, the form and frequency of uterine contractions in labour and delivery, antiperistaltic and retroperistaltic contractions in vomiting, movements and sounds that induce trance states, the activity of pharyngeal and oesophageal muscles in infants' rumination (Gaddini, 2002), all characterized by an *accelerando* that leads to final discharge and relief or fulfilment. In Chapter 1, I already pointed out the possibility that temporal and rhythmic nuclei with a binary structure build up the primal scheme that allows the dawning psyche to signify so far meaningless stimuli. It is a process that can be traced back to prenatal life, when auditive ability largely pre-dates the development of visual perception. Rhythm, and more generally temporality, rooted in the somato-psychic being, alongside sound, are key elements for subjectivity and symbolic functions. Musical symbolism, a *presentational symbolism*, radically differs from image and verbal symbolism: Susanne Langer (1951) highlighted in music the coincidence of form and content, resulting in a *significant form*. As a non-discursive symbolism, independent from words and images (and therefore from word- and thing-presentations), music is untranslatable and, because of that, apt to express what is unspeakable. Music is therefore the primal language that marks the original impact with the world and the psychic experience, joined only later by the word.

The very precocious appearance of the musical presence and modus operandi in psychic functioning and development, together with its primary conditions of motion and plurality of the involved senses, makes highly plausible the assumption of a musical unconscious that coincides with the origin of the unconscious psyche and that, at the same time, has an important role in the outlining of the experiences of space and time. In addition, through motion and sensoriality music is rooted in the whole made up of the mother–infant body and later in the relationships among more than one body, being also a vector of unconscious messages from adults to the *infans*.

From the sound bath to the sound envelope that characterize the infant's early experience of the world, a family musical interpretation of experience takes shape and becomes a source of protection, stimulation and communication with the baby: to this *family vocal group* the infant adds her/his perception of her/his own sound production, thus arriving at diversifying internal and external sound spaces and identifying more than one voice at a time, which is a specific musical competence.

The Noise family

The family setting is vividly impregnated with rhythms, sounds and silences, and with all their possible articulations resulting from the presence of several people at once, with their intrapsychic, interpsychic and interphantasmatic worlds, in the space–time of the setting. The analyst, as a component of the family group, may often face hard times in dealing with interweaving conversations, transitions, breaks, echoes, overlaps, interruptions and fragmentations, to which the varied forms assumed by the infra-verbal, gestural and expressive components must be added, resulting in an increased complexity of verbal and interactive exchanges between members of the group. When we succeed in grasping sound and rhythmic articulations of the verbal language and of the interactions among the family group components, including the analyst, we can get closer to the unconscious formations without figurability that express unthinkable and unspeakable elements but, nevertheless, are able to move and implicate the other.

During the first family session with the Noise family I work hard to follow the unravelling discourses, while nine-year-old Giacomo plays with a big car ('a strange car') that he has assembled with building blocks and hurls at full speed from wall to wall in the consulting room. My difficulty with verbal understanding becomes absolute with regard to Giacomo's utterings: besides the noise he produces, he never directly addresses me (though his father repeatedly exhorts him to turn to me when speaking), but talks with an undefined interlocutor, while keeping to the game of controlling whether the car has lost pieces and passengers during its runs. In the meantime, Mr and Mrs Noise brief me on Giacomo's anxieties, which assault him at the time of going to school or to sleep, or even in social situations that require leaving the parents. They try to bring in the child, who does not escape, but confirms their account.

Verbal discourse conveys the couple's awareness of the difficult effort to combine two contrasting family traditions: in the mother's family of origin a clearly symbiotic quality prevails, which is expulsive of any oedipal articulation and violent through an intrusive and colonizing mother's attitude. The paternal side, conversely, is defined as '*à la Beautiful*', as it is marked by an acrobatic integration of new and old partners, as well as children born from subsequent relationships, who make up a kind of middle generation, without apparent conflicts or ruptures. I feel a huge transgenerational weight burdening the small Noise family, who invested its whole creative potential in an only child and only grandchild for both his biological and acquired grandparents.

Paying close attention to the various levels at which the family discloses itself, I find a clear contrast or juxtaposition of noise and words. It appears more and more distinct that the meaning is not the most important component of these exchanges; there is another level of experience that surfaces in the session, perhaps an indecipherable and pervasive primal scene that disturbs and overpowers intended communications. From another perspective, this family seems to me to be enveloped in a noisy skin, which protects its own contents but also expresses them in a pre-symbolic form: as a result, the other is occupied and is pushed towards an almost symmetrical attitude of self-protection and paralysis. In this communication mode I sense a subject–object confusion that, on the one hand, needs defences to strengthen boundaries but, on the other, is itself a defence against fragmentation anxiety and fear of loss of parts of oneself. The sound discourse appears, therefore, in contradiction with the reassuring account of a triumph over the conditions that were imposed by preceding generations, as well as with the normalizing efforts directed to Giacomo's anxieties, based on reassurance and minimizing.

According to Anzieu (1974, 1985), all individuals have a narcissistic envelope since birth, which he named the Skin-Ego: it is the Ego's metaphoric representation of self as a container of psychic contents, on the basis of the early experience of the body surface. The earliest representation of self is therefore a pre-individual psychic cavity in which unity and identity are only outlined. The skin-Ego is a very complex apparatus with many functions, among which the container, the outside/inside separation, the stimulation and inscription surface. It begins as a phantasy of a shared mother–infant skin that should be tight enough to hold, but should not suffocate idiosyncratic motion and sensitivity that initiate subjectivation processes. The importance ascribed to containers led Anzieu to identify other kinds of envelopes that are built up from different sensorial modalities (sound, visual, olfactive envelopes) and functions (memory, dream). The sound envelope introduces the space dimension (orientation, distance) and temporality. Similarly, Ogden (1989a) focused the primary function of the edge in the dawning psyche and the importance of a sensory skin as a background for the psychic inscription of experience.

With the Noise family we are witnessing the creation of a rough and irksome family sound envelope, that yet proves good at holding and is able to express what otherwise could not be expressed. In this family, Giacomo is the spokesperson for all the members' anxiety and for a shared phantasy of getting lost and falling into the void if primal relationships are de-symbiotized and differentiated. Giacomo shares with his parents motions of intolerance and rebellion that, besides being inconclusive, result in additional undifferentiation of subjects and generations: for any topic concerning or referring to the son, there is always a comment by the mother or the father about her/his having been so or wished the same, while the child often takes upon himself judicial and decision-making functions that invade the field of parental functions.

The appreciation of the communicative function in the session on the part of what at first sight could be viewed as a disruption of communication and an expression of an overflowing and un-integrable drive excess allows the verbal expression both of the impossible project of buying a new home, suited to the family needs and thus breaking free from the family tradition that obliges each new generation to move into the grandparents' home, and of death anxieties or nameless/shapeless dreads that Mr Noise manifests through somatic symptoms that deeply worry him and repeatedly take him to the emergency department.

During the second family session, the noisy game with the car starts again, joined by Giacomo's remark: 'It doesn't make much sense!' The mother, and later the father too, sit on the floor and join in the game of mutually throwing the car about, which loosens the hold of all the car's bits.

Mrs Noise: 'You want to break it up at all costs!'

Giacomo tries to reassemble it, while his father questions him about how school was today, since a teacher was absent. He answers: 'They split us up' (to distribute them into other classes). The car continues to be slammed from one side to the other, but still works even with some pieces missing. Mr Noise observes that it seems an elephant to him, but without a trunk, whereas Mrs Noise says it looks like an Indian totem. Giacomo adds some passengers and, among these, a female doctor, for people falling off the car and getting hurt. When I stress the reference to falling off, separating and getting hurt, like when going to school, to sleep, or moving to a completely new home, and the doctor's role of treating the injured, Giacomo hints at recent conflict with the maternal grandparents and takes the responsibility upon himself. The parents, however, rectify and scale down the extent and duration of the rupture: it was the mother who was angry with them because they criticized the parents' decision of leaving Giacomo alone at home for an hour.

Giacomo introduces a new rule into the game of car throwing, but it is not clear whether it prescribes or forbids touching the wall. The father points out that now the child is going to sleep alone, but Giacomo adds: 'With difficulty…' Mr Noise talks about his son's struggle when going to sleep over or playing team and movement games, but Giacomo complains: 'Why do you have to talk about that? It's only because I'm not so good…'

In the third family session, rage surfaces in Giacomo's accounts about his teachers who scold and yell, and his mother who shouts when she is angry. The car runs over the puppets the mother added to the game, drawing protests from the parents. Here the sound element takes on a different form as it embodies the human voice, whose piercing excess is felt trespassing identity boundaries and killing. Hence, we have moved from the noise, which is produced by inanimate objects, to the voice, which expresses each subject's singular corporeity and carries a pure emotion (rage), not yet signified by the word. The voice, acoustic material that precedes and exceeds language, unveils its closeness to the unconscious and annuls the gap between murderous phantasies and reality.

In the following session, when I meet Giacomo alone, there is a significant passage from the deafening and occlusive noise of the car to a noise that asks to be understood: the boy gets curious at a sort of clicking produced by the turning wheels and looks for its origin: 'I hadn't noticed it before', as if in the session, perhaps because the parents are absent, sounds can surface with a meaning to be discovered, rather than being shapeless and covering noises. The car game changes from the aim of circumventing obstacles, which is not without reference to Giacomo's expectations when he comes to the sessions, to the search for a new balance between the different component blocks, as long as there is always a doctor who can revive injured people, even if she might herself get hurt. Giacomo thereby expresses the death anxieties that all the family members produce. The doctor shocks the wounded: 'It is the only technique I know, hence I always use it', maybe a hint at the rigidity and scarcity of available defences, with an attitude of phobic avoidance of possible new solutions. 'I like it when the watch changes hour', Giacomo remarks after glancing at his watch, and then adds, after some reflection: 'I don't know why, perhaps because the minutes return to the zero'. Here, in the therapeutic situation, we may ask ourselves the meaning of our feelings, which lead us to perceive that we like or do not like something, while a wish to reset the minutes, to start over, is working its way, maybe to resume a not well-defined subjectivation process. This undoubtedly requires a lot of effort, and Giacomo indeed works very hard to replace the top of the car with another block, without openings, and focuses his efforts on welding the blocks together well. Towards the end of the session, Giacomo asks me about the other children who come to me and adds: 'I like being an only child better'. All movements are therefore dangerous, and this is perhaps in relation to the lack of siblings.

In the following family session, the noise that disturbs the conversation reappears, but is less invasive. An occurrence is reported in which, during a visit to a museum, Giacomo switched over his audioguide, thus listening to explanations addressed to other groups or even, according to him, to a radio channel that was broadcasting music: the family music feels unsatisfying, Giacomo looks for something different elsewhere, and discovers that the unidirectional adult–child discourse can disarticulate and open up to larger groups or even turn into music! We are thus confronted with a paradoxical element, a found–created that can be shared in the session as something opposed to what is predefined, and that can be created by the subject in the solitude of his private connection with the audioguide. There is also the experience of one's own subjectivity, to be found when being alone, through receiving music that comes from an unidentifiable elsewhere.

The voice comes back in the account about Giacomo's perception, simply from a change in the father's voice, a tension in him towards his son, doubling the tension between Mr Noise and his mother: a friendly and cheerful grandmother, yet described by the couple as messy and bungling and therefore inclined to upset family balances. The voice gets to convey conflicts and affects from one generation to the next, resulting in a spalling of those contents at a number of levels, conscious and communicable, as well as unconscious and unspeakable. As such, it takes on the function of a memory that is handed on unmodified, and marks off its alterity inside a word that intends to be, in contrast, sympathetic and reassuring.

The confusion between affects and contents belonging to both generations, as well as to different subjects, appears in the father emphasizing Giacomo's surprise during his first communion when he was asked to drink wine; but the boy denies it, thus reversing the situation: he already knew it, whereas his parents were the ones to stay behind and to be surprised. In the meantime, Giacomo is playing with a coin and testing its production of varying noises when rubbed against different materials. While I stress the surfacing of different voices and sounds, Giacomo points out that just at that moment noises were heard like borborygmi, which he locates inside his father's stomach. The father resumes the topic of drowning out noises, relating them to Giacomo's need to protect himself from their pressures: as a young child, he was very stubborn, always had the last word, but they as parents were more indulgent.

As the family work continues, on the one hand the parents report their decision of formulating a purchase proposal for a new house, only to receive a refusal; on the other, Giacomo talks about his new bed and how he slept well, though at night an unusual noise made him immediately think that there was a thief. The family, with Giacomo using the pen, outlines a square on the whiteboard in which the family members gradually come to life and in turn narrate anxious dreams about catastrophic separation and englobing. Noises continue to represent 'bothersome' expressions to be rejected, but they may temporarily also take shape and acquire a potential meaning, as when Giacomo asks his mother to guess what song it is from a rhythm he is producing. On the whiteboard, first the borders of Italy are put to the test by the need to make room for all the Italian regions, then the word *'wolves'* appears, in apparent contradiction to the drawing of the she-wolf with twins Romulus and Remus. While the mother is worried about a marker sign on the wall, left by Giacomo the previous time, as a deforming track on the border of our therapeutic group, the boy appears to stress the noise discriminant function by making the markers screech: 'That doesn't bother you?'

In this family, noise, as opposed to sound, might have taken on the meaning of 'the formless' Fédida (2000) talked about, qualifying it as a movement and process that springs from the deteriorating of the alliance between signifier and signified in words. De-signification and deformation are, after all, the very movements that characterize the psychoanalytic situation, whose onset is marked by the feeling of the uncanny (*unheimlich*) and that hearkens to the sexual excess that is implied in words. As the antelinguistic side of words and the reverse of things, the formless according to Fédida lies in the relationship between things, moves among excesses, lacerations and remains, and puts forms in motion, carrying them away from idealization and abstraction.

Epilogue

Giacomo's absence from the session because of a summer school he did not willingly go to, and the forthcoming summer break appear in the last couple of sessions in the difficult adjustment to silence, which induces deep anxieties but can also open up a potential space of absence. The parents report that Giacomo asked them, as an antidote to the silence of their voices, for a small note written by them to take along with him, and complained about the teachers' scoldings, a jarring element when compared to familiar voices. In this session, the last one before the summer holidays, Mr and Mrs Noise announce their decision to get married, expounding it as a significant separating and subjectivating movement from their families of origin: from the maternal family, governed by the rule that the family of origin must always stick together, leaving the daughters' partners outside the home walls; and from the paternal family, since the couple can allow themselves to aim for a future stable and long-lasting couple relationship. A significant transference component does not fail to involve both the space of the analytic group that could become binding and asphyctic, and the therapeutic relationship's duration, either limited or endless. However, the intention to involve neither witnesses nor guests makes it an almost secret, voidable marriage: this topic takes shape alongside the couple's difficulty to take on a parental function, almost as if marrying, being parents, and buying a home were all direct attacks against their own parents that irremediably deprive and harm them. 'I find it very difficult to outline a perimeter that encloses intimate people; I feel bad about leaving someone out', Mr Noise clarifies. A paralysing hesitation ensues about the date and place of the event, while the couple recalls how much easier it was, particularly for Mr Noise, to decide to have a child. This has to do, therefore, with a resuming of the subjectivation process, *with the minutes returning to the zero*, and the unmasking of a failed establishment of a time and place for the subjects and the couple, viewed as a pluri-subjective whole. The birth of a child to be shared with the grandparents allowed the couple to avoid outlining a perimeter or boundary, namely the dyadic membrane of the couple, with the resulting confusion of generations and the failed establishment of the asymmetry that is implied in the parental function. The marriage plan, however, involves a temporal movement and space definition that, although very difficult, can trigger significant transformation processes in the couple and the family.

Voices, sounds and rhythms in the family unconscious

In the family, as I touched upon at the start of this chapter, the word's phonic component and the voice's bodily substance, as well as the involvement of bodies and objects in the sound product that characterizes their musical form, join the individual and groupal rhythms, thereby making up the specific musical unconscious for each family. Not only intonation and prosody but also the sound shape of words and voice quality convey its unconscious or primal elements, which are part of the newborn's and then the infant's early sensory experience, both through her/his own and familiar people's voices, and through bodily and environmental noises.

Music's polyphonic structure reveals and expresses the simultaneity and complexity of experiences, relationships and unconscious movements that are specific of each subject, but even more specific of groups, and among these, the family. The musical interval, which unites and separates two or more sounds, may be considered the root of human relationality: in addition, unplayed sounds, yet perceptible as harmonically fundamental sounds, perform the basic function of the third, or the unconscious link.

Family temporality originates from rhythm and discontinuity in the subjective experience, and also from historicization that entrenches the family group in a generational past and projects it towards the future of its progeny. Time is therefore not only a structural family component but also a basic organizer of it: family inter-rhythmicity is creatively formed from the different subjective rhythms, synchronic but also heterochronic or dyschronic. This process leads to overcoming what Kaës named *group achrony*, an archaic situation in which the boundaries between individual psychic spaces are cancelled and therefore merge, with an obliteration of differences between different family members' affects and representations. In such circumstances a time without temporality establishes itself, similar to what Anzieu described as a *groupal illusion*, caught between the two extremes of a magic, perfect and motionless omnipotence and the time of annihilating catastrophe and suffering. In order to save the family group unity and coherence, individual temporalities are stifled or nipped in the bud, and the disintegrating threat of differentiation and building of boundaries between individuals and generations nullified. On the other hand, the access to a symbolic time requires an integration of the individual subject's temporality into the group time, without this involving killing oneself or the family group; rather, this involves a possible dyschrony in the groupal time that coincides with the *ability to be alone in the group* (Kaës, 2015). Similarly, the movement of disillusion allows – inside a sound–musical psychic envelope with containing, protecting and communicative functions – individual sound spaces to unfold that are rooted in the primary sound–rhythmical sensations registered in the sound body.

These theoretical considerations and clinical experiences are intended to highlight the musical structure of the family unconscious, which also includes noise, as a group product in which sound and rhythm are not yet structured. Similarly to the process of tonality disintegration in twentieth-century music, which arrived at introducing noise into music, in family and child psychoanalysis noise may take on a key role: rather than amounting to a disturbance in communication, it can become a significant sound component in the intersubjective relationships, apt to be interpreted as a genuine expression of the unconscious, either individual or groupal. In the history of music, this evolution marked the fact that, since Debussy, the harmonic predominance was giving way to timbric specificity that could not allow transcriptions without drastically changing the meaning of the musical piece.

The primary psychic functioning, founded on a mainly sensorimotor and groupal organization, musically represents itself through sensoriality (auditive, tactile, proprioceptive, vibratory) and motion (bodily, rhythmic, of sound waves, of musical flow). It continues to operate all life long, but blossoms in the original exchanges between the foetus or newborn and the parents or the nurturing environment, and in the intersubjective structures that make up groups. In the specific family structure, it is enriched by temporal elements that extend to history and legacies from previous generations and to planning and expectations falling on future generations. In our clinical work with families we can, therefore, benefit from a regredient (and dreaming) listening, ready to be impregnated by inarticulate noises, silences and dysrhythmias, and able to facilitate the unfolding and self-phantasizing of the family's musical unconscious.

> 'Music is perhaps above psychoanalysis. I think, indeed, that there are things that music can express, but that psychoanalysis has not much to say about. In addition, I am convinced that there are analysts who love painting and analysts who love music. They are not interested in the same things. I assume that psychoanalysts who love music are those who consider affect as an essential dimension and could never be satisfied with language games and fascinating stories.' Music meets psychoanalysis 'mainly in rhythm, time and musical phrasing. It is there that music meets psychoanalysis. There is a phrasing, a sort of breathing, that only analysis can give some idea of.'
> (André Green, interviewed by Manuela Trinci, Sentieri Erranti, 2010, author's translation)

Chapter 8

Silence and absence: Sound and music during the coronavirus pandemic

Moving towards the conclusion of this book, I find myself reflecting again upon listening as the main working tool of both music and psychoanalysis. Playing and listening are one; it is impossible to play without listening, both to the sounds played by the listener and those possibly produced by playing partners. Likewise, psychoanalytic listening and communicating are one, since listening is a very active process, a dialectic and intersubjective two-way movement. Psychoanalytic listening, indeed, blends in verbal and non-verbal communication, since it is located in the relationship between analyst and patient/s. Imbued with time and rhythm, in their most intersubjective articulations, psychoanalytic listening has the highest transformative potential.

Perhaps this is one main reason why I was so deeply impressed by the sound and music dimension in the unique experience of the 2020 Coronavirus crisis, which I went through in Italy while it spread worldwide.

During the first days of lockdown in Italy for the COVID-19 pandemic, every day at 6 p.m. people went to the window or stepped out on the balcony, singing or playing music. It was intended to be a moment of playful sharing despite the confinement at home, an opportunity to bring each other comfort and to fill the prescribed distance among people. Strangely enough, 6 p.m. was the time when every day the head of the Italian Civil Protection Department held a TV news conference conveying the numbers of those infected, dead and cured. Consequently, if you were meeting people on the balcony, you could not listen to the news, which was relentlessly worsening day after day.

The lockdown period of almost three months was marked by very strong emotions: anxiety, bewilderment, grief, condolence, boredom, panic, excitement and so on. Depending on our lifestyle, work requirements and relational and family status, we all had to adjust our daily schedule, both in time and mainly in space. As a result, we had to mourn our usual way of living, at the most intimate and personal level as well as in the more social and public dimensions. We lost the concreteness of what appeared to be obvious and of the sensory background that unknowingly we were used to perceiving and breathing in every moment of our life. What had been taken for granted, and therefore had been doomed to remain unchanged, suddenly turned out to be ephemeral: we painfully missed it, but we also felt that perhaps we could do without it, as long as we revised our values and priorities.

Moreover, a common experience that permeated every moment during those days was the dramatic change of the sound environment, mainly in cities. We were used to hearing an unceasing background noise of traffic and nearby or faraway machinery and working tools of all sorts, but now, after a short while, we realized that we could catch human voices at a conversational sound level, birds singing and noises from human activities and movements ... A paradoxical and ominous holiday atmosphere spread throughout our lives without affecting our painful emotions, but rather bringing about a sense of derealization and a feeling of uncanniness.

We were abruptly thrown into a new way of living and relating that required complete avoidance of contact among people, even with our beloved daughters and sons, grandchildren, parents, sisters and brothers, not to mention friends and, as psychoanalysts, our patients. In order to continue our work with them, we mostly turned to technology and experienced, sometimes for the first time, a new kind of analytic relationship, via the telephone, Skype or other videoconferencing platforms. The exchanges of our observations led to discussions about the plausibility of such ways of performing analyses and psychotherapies, in full awareness that they are not equivalent to the traditional mode. The practice of remote sessions was not a choice, the alternative being an open-ended interruption.

In this conclusive chapter, I would like to discuss observations and experiences about these modified forms of life in general and psychoanalytic work in particular: I feel they are of the utmost significance in order to begin the working-through of the traumatic quality of living the pandemic as well as a sort of experimental setting for highlighting key components of our work, such as listening, sensorial envelopes, time, the setting and the voice. Our psychoanalytic work underwent major transformations of the setting and important changes in the sensory environment of the sessions, with major implications for the patient–analyst relationship. Besides such a radical change of the setting, we also had to confront a new form of symmetry as a result of being immersed, just as our patients were, in a new and threatening situation: a traumatic experience extended in time and space without limits.

Living immersed in an ongoing traumatic situation holds us in a present time, as opposed to the *après-coup* time that allows psychic work and elaboration. Likewise, the sound and musical world, in which time processing is crucial, is drastically altered. Nevertheless, the patients' ability to keep dreaming and freely associating shows that the function of the setting, though abruptly changed, has not utterly failed, but still guarantees a reliable and safe-enough (however virtual) space and time.

In remote analysis we are deprived of our senses of touch, smell and taste, while a dominant role is given back to listening, and vision depends on the chosen means of communication (i.e. videoconferencing platforms or WhatsApp as opposed to the telephone). Listening, however, is a complex sense, that involves not only the ear and the related nervous paths and brain areas but also the skin and the whole body, through its vibratory and pressure components. The latter are no longer conveyed through remote communication or, at most, are generated by our computers or mobile phones rather than by our bodies.

When using Skype (or similar alternatives), many functions so far entrusted to the analyst, such as outlining the space of the setting, are now taken on by the patient, who chooses the room in which to welcome the analyst, and the quality and extension of the shown view of the home environment. In this doubled setting, while we offer the patient a glimpse of the familiar space of our office, the view she/he chooses for us comprises personal details (not just belonging to the patient her/himself) and, especially, noises and sounds from the home and its inhabitants or even from the neighbours. When the chosen means is the telephone, we cannot even glean an idea of the patient's part of the setting, though patients often tell us they are in the living room, or bedroom, or rather weird places such as the bathroom or the car, the only place felt safe enough for their privacy. Although patients make more or less effort to isolate the session environment, we can sense the echoes of the family soundtrack they are immersed in and have contributed to create (Lecourt's *bruissement familial*): it is the sound environment in which the patient lives, that now, through our perception, can convey areas otherwise unknowable, at least in such a direct and evident form. The invasiveness of such a sound environment may also, paradoxically, result as deafening, distracting our senses from the task of grasping unconscious derivatives and phantasies.

A young woman in analysis for five years is now taking her sessions via Skype: she lies down on her living-room couch, pointing her mobile phone to the wall and the ceiling so that we meet each other's gaze only at the beginning and the end of the sessions. However, a major change is the constant presence of her dog nearby, though I never see it. When she got it, it was a severely traumatized pooch that never made a sound. Now it takes part in the session, usually through hushed yelps. One of these sessions began with the clear noise of the dog kibble crunching. The patient then related a dream:

She was travelling in a train. She has two backpacks, but only one is hers. When she arrives at her stop, she takes only one backpack and her dog collar. After getting out, she realizes she forgot the second backpack, but what she feels is much more important, she left her dog on the train.

The patient's prevailing, unpleasant feeling appears to result from having lost and missing an essential part of her belongings, among which her most primordial and formless affects. The dog is a real and significant character, present both in the dream (through its absence) and in the reality of the session, though out of my visual field but well perceivable through its voice. Perhaps we can consider it a transitional object in its belonging both to the patient's internal and external worlds. What is marked by the concreteness of a real presence, usually not welcomed in the analytic setting, through the oneiric work becomes a representation, apt to take part in the analytic work and bringing forth feelings of abandonment and guilt, probably related also to the change of setting.

This was not so at the beginning of our change to remote analysis, which apparently jeopardized the psychic and dream work of this patient up to the point of producing bare images of death, unusable for the dreamwork. After a terrible weekend, marked by feelings of agony, this patient had reported the following dream:

I was seeing my father (a doctor who was working in a hospital in the most COVID-affected area of Italy) *lying though not dead. He was sleeping and I was close to him and cried desperately.*

The following night *I woke up screaming, something like a pavor nocturnus, I just cried and trembled, I was terrified.*

A couple of days later, she dreamed again about her father: *I was trying to hug my father, but he was not allowed to. However, I needed to hug him ... In a second dream I am pregnant and I wonder how it is possible, since my boyfriend and I practise the withdrawal method.*

The present situation of banned closeness and contact with other people (confinement) intertwines with her unconscious conflict between Oedipal investment and the related prohibition, which are made real and tangible by the change of setting and of the transference relationship. In the first dream, there is neither separation between subject and object nor distinction between something and its representation (sleeping and being dead, which overlap). As representation becomes possible, as well as awareness of her own needs, there is a shift from vision and listening (seeing her father, crying) into a sense of touch and the perception of distance. Yet, closeness still appears to be inconceivable.

In the following session, she announces she has moved into another room of the house, situated on the lower floor, since her boyfriend needs the living room for a business meeting. She describes it, a pretty, empty room, with its window and view, its colours and its silence, which brings out every slightest noise or sound. She remarks that its good acoustics make it suitable for singing and playing. It used to be a disquieting room, a depository of different, often forgotten things. She also used to perceive its uninhabited space as full of unknown feelings, phantasies, fears. Yet, after her brother occupied it for a few days, she came to consider it as a guestroom, suitable for welcoming friends and relatives. From a visual to a sound and affective space, she is opening this new private space up to the analytic couple.

A week later, there is another dream: *I was travelling on a bus leading to C (a village not far from the city). I would get off on N street, but the bus turns back to the terminal. I ask a female passenger why, because I am worried it will take too long. She answers that the bus must go through the terminal, like a circular bus. It reminds me of the bus I take when I come to your office, it is a circular bus.* At this point, I hear the dog whimpering, as a spokesperson of its owner's pain. The apparent easy compliance by the patient with the new session arrangement appears to be, in fact, very problematic. She questions a female passenger about the length of this unexpected detour, pointing to her perception that in this predicament I am a passenger just like her as well as to her wish to give me the responsibility to take her back to the known track. She cannot voice her own suffering, split and entrusted to her dog.

In these sessions, the dog was always there: I never saw it, but it could always make itself heard through yips and wailings, sometimes very similar to babies' whimpers, apparently connected to the matter in hand.

I am very alerted by the sound dimension of the new setting: besides new noises and sounds from the new character that is the dog, those almost imperceptible body sounds such as breath, movements, borborygmi, always contributing to a lively background to patient's and analyst's utterances and silences, are now mute, sometimes replaced by strange noises produced by computers or phones, often without it being possible to understand their origin: internal vs external, mine vs patient's. Moreover, the dog's voice, as well as that of the cat of another patient, often sharing the home couch with her during our sessions, appears to my ear noticeably distorted, much more than the patients' voices.

Even when the remote sessions perfectly imitate a regular session, the sensorial perception is strongly distorted: images via the screen are flat, bidimensional, though they simulate three-dimensionality, and are made of small particles – pixels – that gather together to offer an illusion of continuity. Faces are deformed, particularly when too close to the camera, but also in their movements and expressions, now and then fixed or slowed down and jerky by an occasional poor connection. The sound of the voice, too, rather than coming from a body with its vocal cords and bodily sounding boards, is the result of a synthesis of sounds produced by the computer or the phone, and often appears to be highly distorted. However, we are used to recognizing familiar voices on the phone, though they are different from directly perceived voices, through the active, auditive work of breaking down and re-synthesizing the sounds we are listening to.

Perhaps all this is implied in the dream reported by another female patient, thirty years old, right after her first session on Skype:

> *I was with my sister (she is in analysis too) in a sort of waiting room, such as in a family doctor's office. Patients were called by an interphone. When we are called, we go in: we see many desks, all alike, with a computer on each of them and a photocopier at the back. Behind one of these desks my sister's analyst is sitting. The three of us have a session: it is weird, I can't get the sense. Then I see a childhood friend of mine, I feel happy and I want to say hallo to him.*

The first Skype session opens a new experiential world, where we share the attitude of waiting, a dominant condition in this time, both within the analytic relationship and the external world. Inside my mind, her claiming sounds like this: 'You can put all the available computers at my disposal, but your voice is no longer the same, and my analyst too is no longer the same! I feel dehumanized, a patient like many others that must wait her turn. Everything looks false, like a copy of our relationship. I am experiencing an uncanny feeling, I would prefer to go back to our familiar world, in which it was just you and me.'

The same patient, who seemingly accepted the change of setting right away, at the first Skype session found herself painfully missing the car trip, the drive over the distance between her home and my office, a frame or transitional space full of thinking, feeling, freely associating, stirred by the forthcoming or by the just occurred session.

The expectation, as well as the wake left at the end, both experienced and acted in the move from one place to another, are always part of the session and play a specific role in outlining the setting and its rhythm. They have the same function as the silence before and after music that makes it possible, and that is also a vital component of it. It is an expression of the work of mourning and of elaborating time, in order to maintain the desire alive, a function that in music is performed by the pauses and particularly by the *fermata* (see figs. 2.2 and 2.3). At the end of a movement of a piece of music, the *fermata*, through lengthening a pause or a sound, marks a time of expectation and uncertainty, suspending us in doubt as to whether the work has come to an end or will start again with either a repetition or a new movement having a whole new development.

Even sporadic, out-of-setting communications, almost accidentally thrown out while entering or leaving the office, are no longer possible: as a result, their function of allusion to or focalizing nodal questions is lost. Without these framing elements, the platform or phone session is felt almost naked, or at least unprepared, and more work is required in order to build it up without feeling invaded by the other or invading him/her. The music of the setting is missing, due to a loss of transitional spaces that by the indefiniteness of inner and outer, and of mine and yours, confer meaning on our experiences, just like the intervals between sounds, in which we perceive movements that are the only source of melodies and harmonies.

From another analysis, recently started with a man in his fifties, two dreams were related during the first Skype session. In the first one, *I am in my parents' house, where a festive atmosphere reigns. On a bed I see a butchered lamb, with its raw flesh, a very big one. Somebody cuts it up, I don't know whether it's me or somebody else ... then there is one more scene: a piglet is running through the hallway and slipping on the floor. My children with their cousins are laughing. They put carpets and sheets of paper down to stop the piglet from slipping.*

In the second dream, *I am waiting to leave with my wife and daughter; I say I'll get going. I am driving a Cinquecento, but then I think I would rather wait for them. I find myself driving around an unusual square, which lies upon a tunnel, with a difference in height so that I can't drive round in circles as I thought, but forming a figure 'eight'. They arrive later on, and are riding horses: my daughter's horse, a black one, trips over a cobblestone and falls down, stiffly overturning on its side. My daughter gets up, she has suffered no physical injury.*

The first dream begins with a return to the reassuring and safe environment of the childhood home. The violent irruption of animal characters into a familial, festive situation may allude to the catastrophic change of setting, allowing my abrupt and excessive irruption into the patient's familial environment. The festive, honeymoon atmosphere of the just started analysis is disrupted by the bloody image of a butchered lamb and the grotesque scene of the slipping piglet. Incertitude rules about who is taking apart the just built-up setting: him or me? And whether the piglet will get hurt or amuse the children. In the second dream the wait that characterizes these days is evoked again (as by the second patient I mentioned), but is unbearable for the patient, driving him to leave alone. A similar circular motion is described here as in my first patient's dream of the bus: a closed figure that in this last dream partially opens into a figure 'eight'. The circle appears as a protective, enveloping and regressive form as opposed to the traumatic situation that destroys the protective envelope, leaving the subject naked, similar to the platform sessions in which the second patient feels deprived of the trip there and back. But what I perceive with marked intensity in these dreams is the sensorial element: the horrific and unexpected vision of the butchered lamb and the act of ripping it apart, with the sound of the blade and the smell of the blood, the noise of the piglet's feet slipping on the floor, changed or muffled by the paper or the cloth, the sound of the laughing children, the interoceptive and proprioceptive sensations of height changes and of motion, the sound of galloping and falling down horses ...

Uncanny feelings are stirred by these dream experiences in which something familiar and something apparently new, or weird, are associated. As a matter of fact, this is how dreams usually work: perhaps this is the reason why they are so flourishing in this conjuncture, offering more than one level of understanding, but inevitably referring to the catastrophic transformation of the analytic relationship and setting. However, traumata are characterized by an impairment of both the symbolizing function and the temporal dimension, which implies a stop of psychic work: repression, too, becomes impossible, since it needs the operation of a representative function, involving condensation, displacement and figurability.

Moreover, these dreams perform a traumatolytic function (Ferenczi, 1931), opening the way to the work of mourning of the familiar relationship with the analyst on one hand, and to the symbolization of a traumatic, indigestible reality, marked by pre-symbolic and preverbal mnestic traces on the other. According to Ferenczi, in traumatolytic dreams, the body, in which the traumatic traces are inscribed as bodily memories (memories without recollection), presents through sensoriality and bodily experiences what is to be transformed into thought and language expression. In the sequence of dreams reported by the first patient, beginning with the prevalence of emotions of terror without content, and bodily reactions such as paralysis, tremor, pain and crying, we can recognize Ferenczi's differentiation between primary and secondary dreams: these dreams also point to the patient's traumatic experiences dating back to her infancy, marked by intersubjectivity.

In the same way, as silence facilitates the perception of unusual sounds and noises, the change of setting opens up new dimensions of the encounter for us and, through absence and lack, makes us aware of aspects that we used to take for granted and hence escaped working-through. In this respect, Bleger (1967) addressed the non-dialectic aspects of the analytic situation, distinguishing a processual and a not-processual component of the setting, the latter being the depository of 'the most primitive and undifferentiated organization' (ibid., p. 230).

He concludes that the setting is 'the most primitive part of the personality, the ego-body-world fusion' (ibid., p. 235), resulting from the original fusion with the mother's body. Deprivation inherent in the change of setting may therefore become either utterly destructive or a facilitator of the analytic process.

One more situation that has characterized this pandemic time was the emergency remote counselling service that was activated in many countries: most of the users, when asked, expressed a strong preference for the telephone rather than videoconferencing platforms or similar mediums. A very important element in these circumstances is the rule of giving an appointment, albeit by phone, that preserves the temporal component of the setting: as a result, the encounter is enclosed between a waiting time and a reverberation and elaboration time following the session. When the sessions are more than one, they take on a rhythm that is neither the analyst's nor the patient's, but a third one, resulting from the intersubjective time. Moreover, in this case we do not have to meet a sensorial deprivation as with our usual patients and, moreover, the mourning dimension of the lost relationship and place is lacking. The analyst's voice takes on all the components of the psychoanalytic situation and becomes setting, relationship, listening and response. Patient and analyst will never know the original sound and timbre of each other's voice, though their perceived voices fully take on the function of carrier of the unconscious and the infantile, in their very exceeding and untameable potentialities. And, in my experience, the listening quality of the analyst's voice, with or without actual uttered interventions, can impress a deep and unexpected transforming motion. It is an elaborative listening, in which the analyst's words work more as a stimulus or accomplishment of the subject's own explorative path than as a transforming tool per se.

The very specific, extreme situation of the COVID-19 pandemic highlights the key function of sound, rhythm, listening and voice in the analytic relationship and work. Music, as an essential component of psychic life and work, turns out to be a powerful ally when two or more psyches meet and, more specifically, when a relationship of cure unfolds.

Afterword

Reading this book by Ludovica Grassi took me on a real discovery that filled me with admiration, not only for the depth of the themes treated but also for their originality.

For many years I have been aware of Ludovica's passion for music and her talents as a musician and pianist and I think this book represents a perfect conjunction of her artistic interests and her observational skills as a scholar and clinician.

For some years now many analysts have been involved in working with the primitive states of the mind, the final frontier in the treatment of the most serious cases, for whom the capacity for representation is profoundly limited and the traumata underlying them are unthinkable.

In his book *Feeling the Words* (2004), the Italian analyst Mauro Mancia emphasized the importance of the 'tone, timbre and volume of the voice, and the rhythm, stresses, syntax and timing of the language' (p. 54), whose origins are located in the non-repressed unconscious in the pre-verbal phase of early infancy.

I would particularly like to draw attention to one of the many significant aspects of Ludovica Grassi's book: the author's attentive examination of the sensorial dimensions bound up with sound that particularly impresses the reader for the accuracy of the issues dealt with and the breadth and originality of the bibliography. Research in this field was initiated some time ago, with the first works of Suzanne Maiello (1993) on the sound object as 'the ensemble of the prenatal reminiscences, sonorous and rhythmic quality that the child keeps in his memory after birth, including the mother's voice' and even earlier than that with Didier Anzieu's significant work of 1985 describing the existence of an audio–phonic skin at the start of life and the mother's sound mirror.

Anzieu's 1976 concept of the 'sound envelope' is extremely interesting for psychology and psychoanalysis because it is composed of two complementary facets, a verbal side turned towards the external and a musical side turned towards the internal.

I like to think that they will remain like this for the whole of our life, allowing us to preserve that drive towards the primal music of our intrauterine bond with the mother, a lost paradise that we constantly seek as an aspiration within us under the illusion that one day it will be possible to reach.

It is not by chance that the newborn can immediately distinguish her/his mother's voice from among many others, which has a calming effect on her/him. It is astonishing to observe how she/he will turn in the direction of her voice, picking it out from among others. This sphere of clinical practice and research is growing rapidly, and has now been embraced by the neurosciences too.

Apart from a few exceptions, among which the works I mentioned above, psychoanalysis has, instead, favoured the iconic model. Images have made up the backbone of psychoanalytic studies, starting with the work on dreams. Besides, Freud himself, in 'The Moses of Michelangelo', stated:

> … works of art do exercise a powerful effect on me, especially those of literature and sculpture, less often of painting. This has occasioned me, when I have been contemplating such things, to spend a long time before them trying to apprehend them in my own way, i.e., to explain to myself what their effect is due to. Wherever I cannot do this, as for instance with music, I am almost incapable of obtaining any pleasure. Some rationalistic, or perhaps analytic, turn of mind in me rebels against being moved by a thing without knowing why I am thus affected and what it is that affects me.
> (Freud, 1914, p. 211)

Perhaps this path marked out by Freud has weighed too heavily on the subsequent evolution of psychoanalytic research, although his self-critical confession about his 'rationalistic, or perhaps analytic, turn of mind' and the extent this was contrary to the emotion a piece of music can arouse in us can only prompt our admiration.

And so the story of Narcissus, the young man who gazes endlessly at his reflection, has been the preferred myth among many to interest psychoanalysis, while his musical equivalent, the nymph Echo, has been awarded much less attention. And yet Echo's end, metamorphosed into a rock, illustrates how the missing primitive mirroring that Echo should have received from a loved voice that was not the self literally turns her to stone, transforming her into a lifeless object. Such dynamics demonstrate how psychotic petrification has a primitive origin in the missing musical mirroring of the other, whose first voice belongs to the mother.

We can also see how the analyst's mental states respond not only to the content of what the patient communicates but also to the musicality of the phrasing.

The fact is that, following Anzieu, the musical side turned towards the internal opens up extraordinary, still unexplored clinical and research paths that have a completely different grammar and syntax from those to which we are accustomed: rules that appertain to rhythms, pauses, tones and pitches that we have only recently begun to peek into.

Ludovica Grassi's in-depth research shows us how the basis of the child's symbolic capacity is, therefore, to be rooted not only in visual experiences, as many analysts have affirmed, but much earlier in the 'sound bath' (Anzieu, 1976) in which the foetus, and then the baby, is immersed from five months of intrauterine life onwards.

These memories are then articulated with sounds that the baby produces and that in this way create the first psychic space. The proposal advanced by Ludovica's book allows us to understand how 'the experience of listening to oneself as a source of sounds, as well as the proprioceptive perception of one's own movements and bodily positions in space, comes long before the awareness of oneself as a visual object of the other (mirroring)' (Chapter 2) and, above all, it is the first nucleus of the self.

These observations furnish a hugely significant observational and conceptual revolution reinforcing the empirical observations that many analysts have made during the treatment of seriously disturbed patients. For example, how the tone of voice or the rhythm of words are able to communicate messages that are far more powerful and therapeutic than the contents of those same words. Naturally this involves the person of the analyst and his/her emotional experience to a much greater degree and in a much clearer and more profound way, together, of course, with the relationship he/she is able to co-build with the patient, whose therapeutic efficacy appears increasingly evident. As the mother is capable of communicating profound and intense meanings to her child even before she/he knows how to talk or to understand the meanings of words, merely through what has for some years been called 'motherese' (which, incidentally, used to be called 'baby talk'), that musical babbling between mother and baby, so the analyst must increasingly consider the musicality of his/her words to the patient.

Mauro Mancia observed 'the isomorphism between transferal, poetic and musical language and the unconscious emotional structure of the poet and the speaker' (Giordo, 2020, p. 54, author's translation).

This concerns the person of the analyst because such a level of communication cannot be constructed merely professionally through the use of techniques, however sophisticated. At times we have wondered whether the work of the analyst were an art or a technique and increasingly, thanks to studies such as the one we are now reading, it would appear to be an art with all the subjectivity, specificity and uniqueness of art, tied to the original and creative aspects of the analyst who, like painters, sculptors or musicians, uses the techniques learned during training but then transforms them in tune with his/her personality and spontaneity.

Concerning this point, Ludovica Grassi in fact expounds in these pages on the 'infra-verbal aspects' of the interpretation that can offer 'an expressive configuration of the patient's unconscious contents that are far from the representative level'. And more precisely: 'The musical element, an early primal quality of language, fusing together action, emotion and proto-thought into an undifferentiated whole, enables one to go beyond understanding of the communicated contents and thus open up to participation and a shared experience' (Chapter 1).

Finally, if the foetus already begins to perceive the sound of its mother from the fifth month of pregnancy onwards, it will begin to perceive time too. This is one of the leitmotifs that runs through the work of Ludovica Grassi, to whom we may address just one slight grievance: namely, for having condensed two books in one, for having given us such a treasure trove of research, material and observations that we will have to read the book twice; first to take it all in and digest it and then to delve into the manifold reflections that open up so many innovative trajectories.

One of these certainly concerns time. We can say that the subject of time is psychoanalytical by definition.

The Ego is a store of memories; the question of the *après-coup* is a fundamental theme of psychoanalysis; the unconscious is atemporal; both the analytic process and the session per se are articulations of time. In addition, the experience of subjectivation and becoming a subject is the final point of arrival of a long temporal process.

As Ludovica illustrates for us, music is a succession of tempi, in which the first is abandoned in order to take on the second. Rhythm, melody, harmony and silence characterize the psychic life of the foetus, the newborn, the analyst's interventions and the setting too. We could say that they are sorts of interactions articulated in time and therefore a story of temporal successions and interactions among them.

The author then perspicaciously links these considerations to clinical practice, as we can see in the case of Cosimo where the problem is seen as 'dyschrony and dislocation', terms that 'qualify a very precocious distortion of the organization of somato-psychic functions that unfold through temporal and spatial processes' (Chapter 2).

We have long known that one of the causes triggering psychic collapse is the incapacity to integrate new bodily sensations, for example in the case of the adolescent, with the primitive, archaic, neonatal sensations. These ruptures influence the primitive nucleus of the self. The research expounded in this book specifically stimulates further study into rhythm and musicality, into the musical sensations that are precociously disturbed in the relationship between foetus, baby and mother.

In the timeless unconscious, archaic sensations linger in search of integration thanks to an act of mirroring. The traumatic clash of the past, ever present within us, causes collapse when it encounters new sensations.

New paths open up or old ones are better identified also in terms of acoustic sensoriality in clinical work, and musical considerations naturally take us back to the meaning of time, an exquisitely human event, which originates in the mind of man and for which there is no objective measure.

Anna Maria Nicolò

References

Ajuriaguerra J. de. (1959). *L'Entraînement psychophysiologique par la relaxation.* Paris: Expansion Scientifique.

André J. (2009). 'L'événement et la temporalité. L'après-coup dans la cure'. *Revue française de psychanalyse*, 5, 73: 1285–1352; trans. by Aurora Gentile as 'Evento e temporalità. L'après-coup nella cura'. In Balsamo M. (ed.), *Forme dell'après-coup.* Milan: FrancoAngeli, 2009.

Anzieu D. (1974). 'Le moi-peau'. *Nouvelle Revue de Psychanalyse*, 9: 195–203.

Anzieu D. (1976). 'L'enveloppe sonore du Soi'. *Nouvelle Revue de Psychanalyse*, 13: 161–180.

Anzieu D. (1979). 'The sound image of the self'. *The International Review of Psycho-Analysis*, 6: 23–36.

Anzieu D. (1985). *Le moi peau.* Paris: Dunod; trans. by C. Turner as *The Skin Ego*. New Haven: Yale University Press, 1989.

Anzieu D. (1987). 'Les signifiants formels et le Moi-Peau'. In Anzieu D. et al. (ed.), *Les enveloppes psychiques.* Paris: Dunod, 1987; trans. by Daphne Briggs as 'Formal signifiers and the ego-skin'. In Anzieu D. et al., Psychic Envelopes. London: Karnac Books, 1990.

Arom S. (2000). 'Prolegomena to a biomusicology'. In Wallin N. L., Merker B., Brown S. (eds.), *The Origins of Music*. Cambridge, MA: MIT Press.

Attali J. (1977). *Bruits: essai sur l'economie politique de la musique*. Paris: PUF; trans. by Brian Massumi as Noise: *The Political Economy of Music*. Minneapolis: University of Minnesota Press, 1985.

Aulagnier P. (1975). *La violence de l'interprétation: du pictogramme à l'énoncé*. Paris: PUF, Le fil rouge; trans. by Alan Sheridan as The *Violence of Interpretation. From Pictogram to Statement*. London: Routledge, 2001.

Balestriere L. (1998). *Freud et la question des origins*. Brussels: De Boeck Université.

Balsamo M. (2009). 'Come si traduce Nachträglichkeit in italiano?' In Balsamo M. (ed.), *Forme dell'après-coup*. Milan: Franco Angeli, 2009.

Barale F. (2008). 'Alle origini della psicoanalisi. Freud, Lipps e la questione del "sonoro-musicale"'. *Rivista di Psicoanalisi*, 54: 129–148.

Barale F., Minazzi V. (2008). 'Off the beaten track: Freud, sound and music. Statement of a problem and some historico-critical notes'. *International Journal of Psychoanalysis*, 89: 937–957.

Baruzzi A. (1985). 'Sul ritmo'. *Rivista di Psicoanalisi*, 31: 247–252.
Berio L. 2006. *Un ricordo al futuro. Lezioni americane*. Turin: Einaudi.
Bick E. (1964). 'Notes on infant observation in psychoanalytic training'. *International Journal of Psychoanalysis*, 45: 558–566.
Bick E. (1968). 'The experience of the skin in early object relations'. *International Journal of Psychoanalysis*, 49: 558–566.
Bion W. R. (1965). *Transformations: Change from Learning to Growth*. London: W. Heinemann Medical Books Limited.
Bleger J. (1967). *Simbiosis y ambigüedad: estudio psicoanalitico*. Buenos Aires: Paidós; trans. by John Churcher, Leopoldo Bleger, Susan Rogers as Symbiosis and Ambiguity: A Psychoanalytical Study. London Taylor & Francis, 2013.
Bloom H. (1994). *The Western Canon: The Books and School of the Ages*. New York: Harcourt Brace.
Botella C. (2014). 'On remembering: the notion of memory without recollection'. *International Journal of Psychoanalysis*, 95: 911–936.
Botella C., Botella S. (2001). *La figurabilité psychiche*. Paris: Delachaux et Niestlé; trans. by Andrew Weller as The Work of Psychic Figurability. Mental States without Representation. Hove and New York: Brunner & Routledge, 2005.
Brandt P. A. (2009). 'Music and how we become human – a view from cognitive semiotics. Exploring imaginative hypotheses'. In Malloch S., Trevarthen C. (eds.), *Communicative Musicality: Exploring the Basis of Human Companionship*. Oxford: Oxford University Press.
Brault A., Marty F. (2018). 'L'identité sonore à l'adolescence'. *Adolescence*, 36, 2: 319–331.
Brecht, B. (1961). *Flüchtlingsgespräche*. Berlin: Suhrkamp Verlag; trans. by Romy Fursland as Refugee Conversations, York: Methuen Drama, 2019.
Brown S. (2000). 'The "musilanguage" model of music evolution'. In Wallin N. L., Merker B., Brown S. (eds.), *The Origins of Music*. Cambridge, MA: MIT Press.
Brunello M. (2014). *Silenzio*. Bologna: Il Mulino.
Busoni F. (1907). *Entwurf einer neuen Ästhetik der Tonkunst*. Trieste: Schmidl; trans. by Theodore Baker as Sketch of a New Esthetic of Music. New York: G. Schirmer, 2011.
Busoni F. (1922). *Von der Einheit der Musik [Wesen und Einheit der Musik]*. Berlin: Max Hesses Verlag; trans. by Rosamond Ley as The Essence of Music and Other Papers. New York: Dover Publications, 1957.
Cheung V. K. (2000). 'Bach the transcriber: his organ concertos after Vivaldi'. Available at: http://web.mit.edu/ckcheung/www/MusicalWritings_files/Essay13_BachVivaldiTrans_webversion.pdf (accessed 7June2020).
Ciccone A., Mellier D., Athanassiou-Popesco C., Carel A., Dubinsky A., Guedeney A. (2007). *Le bébé et le temps. Attention, rythme et subjectivation*. Paris: Dunod.
Cismaresco A. S. (1993). 'Le cri néonatal et ses fonctions'. In Busnel M. C. (ed.), *Le langage des bébés*. Paris: J. Grancher, 1993, pp. 253–266.
Cocteau J. (1918). *Le Coq et l'Arlequin. Notes autour de la musique*. Paris: Éditions de la Sirène; trans. by Rollo H. Myers as Cock and Harlequin: Notes Concerning Music. London: The Egoist Press, 1921.
Conrotto F. (2011). 'Ripensare la sessualità infantile'. *Rivista di Psicoanalisi*, 57: 569–585.

Deleuze G. (1968). *Différence et Répétition*. Paris: PUF; trans. by Paul Patton as *Difference and Repetition*. London: Continuum, 2004.

De M'Uzan M. (1970). 'The same and the identical'. *The Psychoanalytic Quarterly*, 76, 4: 1205–1220.

Di Benedetto A. (2000). *Prima della parola. L'ascolto psicoanalitico del non detto attraverso le forme dell'arte*. Milan: Franco Angeli; trans. by Giuseppina Antinucci as Before Words: Psychoanalytic Listening to the Unsaid Through the Medium of Art. London: Free Association Books, 2005.

Dissanayake E. (2000). 'Antecendents of temporal arts in early mother-infant interaction'. In Wallin N. L., Merker B., Brown S. (eds.), *The Origins of Music*. Cambridge, MA: MIT Press.

Estellon V. (2007). 'Écouter, interpréter avec Pierre Fédida'. In Fédida P. (ed.), *Humain/Désumain. Pierre Fédida, la parole de l'œuvre*. Paris: PUF, 2007.

Feder S. (1982). 'The nostalgia of Charles Ives: an essay in affects and music'. *Annual of Psychoanalysis*, 10: 301–332.

Feder S. (1993). 'A tale of two fathers: Bach and Mozart'. In Feder, Karmel and Pollok, 1993.

Feder S., Karmel R. L., Pollok G. H. (eds). (1993). *Psychoanalytic Explorations in Music*. Madison, CT: International Universities Press, 2nd series.

Fédida P. (1995). *Le site de l'étranger: La situation psychanalytique*. Paris: PUF.

Fédida P. (2000). *Par où commence le corps humain. Retour sur la régression*. Paris: PUF.

Fédida P. (2012). *Aprire la parola. Scritti 1968–2002*. Rome: Borla.

Feld S. (1990). *Sound and Sentiment: Birds, Weeping, Poetics, and Song in Kaluli Expression*. Philadelphia: University of Pennsylvania Press.

Feld S. (1994). 'From ethnomusicology to echo-muse-ecology: Reading R. Murray Schafer in the Papua New Guinea Rainforest'. *The Soundscape Newsletter*, 8 June: 9–13.

Feld S. (2003). 'A rainforest acoustemology'. In Bull M. and Back L. (eds.), *The Auditory Culture Reader*. Oxford: Berg, 2003.

Feld S. (2017). 'On post-ethnomusicology alternatives: acoustemology'. In Giannattasio F. and Giuriati G. (eds.), *Perspectives on a 21st Century Comparative Musicology: Ethnomusicology or Transcultural Musicology?* Udine: Nota, pp. 82–98.

Ferenczi S. (1931). 'Gedanken über das Trauma'. *Internationale Zeitschrift für Psychoanalyse*, 1934, XX: 5–12; trans. by E. Mosbacher et al. as 'Reflections on trauma'. In Balint M. (ed.), *Final Contributions to the Problems and Methods of Psychoanalysis*. London: Hogarth, 1955.

Fornari F. (1984). *Psicoanalisi della musica*. Milan: Longanesi.

Freeman W. (2000). 'A neurobiological role of music in social bonding'. In Wallin N. L., Merker B., Brown S. (eds.), *The Origins of Music*. Cambridge, MA: MIT Press.

Freud S. (1895). Project for a scientific psychology. *SE*, 1: 283–387.

Freud S. (1904). 'On psychotherapy'. *SE*, 7: 255–268.

Freud S. (1914). 'The Moses of Michelangelo'. *SE*, 13: 290–238.

Freud S. (1915). 'On transience'. *SE*, 14: 303–307.

Freud S. (1920). 'Beyond the pleasure principle'. *SE*, 18: 1–64.

Freud S. (1921). 'Group psychology and the analysis of the ego'. *SE*, 18: 65–144.

Freud S. (1925a). 'A note upon the "mystic writing-pad"'. *SE*, 19: 225–232.
Freud S. (1925b). 'Negation'. *SE*, 19: 233–240.
Freud S. (1954). 'Letter 52 to Fliess, Dec. 6th'. In Freud S. (1887–1902). *The Origins of Psychoanalysis. Letters to Wilhelm Fliess, Drafts and Notes: 1887–1902*. In Bonaparte M., Freud A. and Kris E. (eds); trans. by Eric Mosbacher and James Strachey. New York: Basic Books, 1954, pp. 173–181.
Freud S. (1954). The Origins of Psychoanalysis. Letters to Wilhelm Fliess, Drafts and Notes: 1887–1902. In Bonaparte M., Freud A. and Kris E.(eds); trans. by Eric Mosbacher and James Strachey. New York: Basic Books.
Freud S. (1929). 'Letter from Sigmund Freud to Ludwig Biswanger, April 11, 1929'. In Freud, E. L. (ed.); trans. by Tania and James Stern as *Letters of Sigmund Freud, 1873–1939*. London: The Hogarth Press, 1961.
Gaddini E. (2002). 'La ruminazione nell'infanzia' (1959) and 'Note sul problema mente-corpo' (1980). In Gaddini E. (ed.), *Scritti, 1953–1985*. Milan: Cortina.
Freud S. (1940). 'An outline of psychoanalysis'. *SE*, 23: 139–207
Gaddini E. (1968). 'Sulla imitazione'. *Rivista di Psicoanalisi*, 14, 3: 235–260.
Gaddini E. (1969). 'On imitation'. *International Journal of Psychoanalysis*, 50: 475–484.
Gaddini E. (1977). 'Formazione del padre e scena primaria'. *Rivista di Psicoanalisi*, XXIII, 2: 157–183.
Galiani R. (2012). 'Introduzione'. In Fédida P. (ed.), *Aprire la parola. Scritti 1968–2002*. Rome: Borla.
Gallese V. (2007). 'Dai neuroni specchio alla consonanza intenzionale. Meccanismi neurofisiologici dell'intersoggettività'. *Rivista di Psicoanalisi*, 53: 197–208.
Gallese V. (2009a). 'Mirror neurons, embodied simulation, and the neural basis of social identification'. *Psychoanalytic Dialogues*, 19: 519–536.
Gallese V. (2009b). 'We-ness. Embodied simulation and psychoanalysis. Reply to commentaries'. *Psychoanalytic Dialogues*, 19: 580–584.
Giordo G. (2020). 'La poetica della parola psicoanalitica'. *Rivista di Psicoanalisi*, LXVI, 1: 53–71.
Graf M. (1947). *From Beethoven to Schostakovich: The Psychology of the Composition Process*. New York: Philosophical Library.
Green A. (1993). *Le travail du négatif*. Paris: Minuit; trans. by Andrew Weller as *The Work of the Negative*. London: Free Association Books, 1999.
Green A. (2000). *Le temps éclaté*. Paris: Minuit; trans. by Andrew Weller as *Time in Psychoanalysis. Some Contradictory Aspects*. London: Free Association Books, 2002.
Green A. (2001). 'Mythes et réalités sur le processus psychanalytique'. *Revue Française Psychosomatique*, 19: 57–88.
Green A. (2002). *Idées directrices pour une psychanalyse contemporaine: méconnaissance et reconnaissance de l'Inconscient*. Paris: PUF; trans. by Andrew Weller as *Key Ideas for a Contemporary Psychoanalysis. Misrecognition and Recognition of the Unconscious*. London: Routledge and the Institute of Psychoanalysis, 2005.
Hanslick E. (1854). *Vom Musikalisch Schönen*. Leipzig: Rudolf Weigel; trans. by Gustav Cohen as *The Beautiful in Music*. New York: The Liberal Arts Press, 1957.
Heidegger M. (1925). *Geschichte des Zeitbegriffs*. P. Jaeger (ed.). Frankfurt/Main: Klostermann, 1979; trans. by T. Kisiel as *History of the Concept of Time*. Bloomington: Indiana University Press, 1985.

Imberty M. (2002). 'La musica e l'inconscio'. In Nattiez J. J. (ed.), *Enciclopedia della Musica. II. Il sapere musicale*. Turin: Einaudi, 2002, pp. 335–360.

Jullien F. (2013). *De l'intime. Loin du bruyant Amour*. Paris: Grasset.

Kaës R. (2015). *L'extension de la psychanalyse. Pour une métapsychologie de troisième type*. Paris: Dunod.

Kahn L. (2012). *L'écoute de l'analyste. De l'acte à la forme*. Paris: PUF.

Kierkegaard S. (1843a). *Enten-Eller*. Copenhagen: C. A. Reitzel; trans. by Howard and Edna Hong as *Either/Or, Part I. Kierkegaard's Writings, III*. Princeton, NJ: Princeton University Press, 1988.

Kierkegaard S. (1843b). *Gjentagelsen*. Copenhagen: C. A. Reitzel; trans. by Howard and Edna Hong as *Repetition* (by Constantin Constantius) in *Fear and Trembling and Repetition*. Princeton, NJ: Princeton University Press, 1983.

Kirkpatrick R. (1935). *The 'Goldberg' Variations*. New York: Schirmer's Library of Musical Classics.

Kohut H., Levarie S. (1950). 'On the enjoyment of listening to music'. *The Psychoanalytic Quarterly*, 19: 64–87.

Kühl O. (2007). *Musical Semantics*. European Semiotics, vol. 7. Bern: Peter Lang.

Lambertucci-Mann S. (2018). 'Vicissitudes des transformations psychique. Le travail de la déformation'. 78ème Congrès des Psychanalystes de langue Française. Genoa, May 10–13, ms.

Langer S. (1942). *Philosophy in a New Key*. Cambridge MA: Harvard University Press.

Langer S. (1951). *Philosophy in a New Key: A Study in the Symbolism of Reason, Rite and Art*. Cambridge, MA: Harvard University Press.

Laplanche J. (1987). *Nouveaux fondements pour la psychanalyse*. Paris: PUF; trans. by David Macey as *New Foundations for Psychoanalysis*. Oxford: Basil Blackwell, 1991.

Laplanche J. (1989). 'Temporalité et traduction: pour une remise au travail de la philosophie du temps'. *Psychanalyse à l'université*, 53: 17–35; trans. by T. Thomas as 'Temporality and translation: for a return to the question of the philosophy of time'. *Stanford Literary Review*, 6, 2(1989): 241–259.

Laplanche J. (1992). *La révolution copernicienne inachevée (Travaux 1967–1992)*, Paris: Aubier.

Laplanche J. (1999). *Entre séduction et inspiration: l'homme*. Paris: PUF; trans. by Jeffrey Mehlman as *Between Seduction and Inspiration: Man*. New York: The Unconscious in Translation, 2015.

Laplanche J. (2006). *Après coup. Problematiques VI*. Paris: PUF; trans. by Jonathan House and Luke Thurston as *Après-coup*. New York: The Unconscious in Translation, 2017.

Lecourt E. (1994). *L'expérience musicale. Résonances psychanalytiques*. Paris: L'Harmattan.

Lecourt E. (2006). *Le sonore et la figurabilité*. Paris: L'Harmattan.

Lecourt E. (2011). 'L'intervalle musical: entre l'Autre et l'autre'. *Insistance*, 2, 6: 119–132.

Lévi-Strauss C. (1964). *Mithologiques*, vol. 1. Paris: Plon.

Lipps T. (1926). *Grundtatsachen des Seelenlebens*. Bonn: Cohen, 1912; trans. by H. C. Sanborn as *Psychological Studies*. USA, Baltimore: The William and Wilkins Company, 1926.

Maiello S. (1993). 'L'oggetto sonoro. Un'ipotesi sulle radici prenatali della memoria uditiva'. *Richard e Piggle*, 1: 31–47.

Maiello, S. (1995). 'The sound-object: A hypothesis about prenatal auditory experience and memory'. *Journal of Child Psychotherapy*, 21, 1: 23–41.
Maiello, S. (2011). 'Dialoghi antelitteram. Note sugli elementi ritmici e sonori del linguaggio e della comunicazione verbale'. *Richard e Piggle*, 19, 3: 246–266.
Maiello, S. (2013). 'On the origins of language. Vocal and rhythmic aspects of the primary relationship and its absence in autistic states.' *Controversy in Children and Adolescent Psychoanalysis*, 13: 23–51.
Malloch S., Trevarthen C. (eds.) (2009). *Communicative Musicality: Exploring the Basis of Human Companionship*. Oxford: Oxford University Press.
Mancia M. (1998). 'Riflessioni psicoanalitiche sul linguaggio musicale'. In Carollo R. ed., *Psicoanalisi e musica*. Bergamo: Moretti e Vitali.
Mancia M. (2004). Sentire le parole. Archivi sonori della memoria implicita e musicalità del transfert. Turin: Bollati Boringhieri; trans. by Judy Baggot as *Feeling the Words: Neuropsychoanalytic Understanding of Memory and the Unconscious*. Hove: Routledge, 2007.
Masson J. M. (ed. and trans.). (1985). *The Complete Letters of Sigmund Freud to Wilhelm Fliess 1887–1904*. Cambridge, MA: Belknap Press.
Meltzer D. (1975a). 'Adhesive identification'. *Contemporary Psychoanalysis*, 11: 289–310.
Meltzer D. (1975b). 'Dimensionality in mental functioning'. In Melzer D., Bremner J., Hoxter S., Weddell D. Wittenberg I., *Explorations in Autism*. Strath Tay: Clunie Press, 1975.
Meltzer D., Harris M. (1976). *The Educational Role of the Family. A Psychoanalytical Model*. London: Karnac, 2013.
Merker B. (2000). 'Synchronous chorusing and human origins'. In Wallin N. L., Merker B., Brown S. (eds.), *The Origins of Music*. Cambridge, MA: MIT Press.
Midolo E. D. (2008). *Sound Matters. Orizzonti sonori della cultura contemporanea*. Milan: Vita e Pensiero.
Mila M. (1963). *Breve storia della musica*. Turin: Einaudi.
Molino J. (2000). 'Toward an evolutionary theory of music and language'. In Wallin N. L., Merker B., Brown S. (eds.), *The Origins of Music*. Cambridge, MA: MIT Press.
Moore J. M., Woolley S. M. N. (2019). 'Emergent tuning for learned vocalizations in auditory cortex'. *Nature Neuroscience*, 22: 1469–1476.
Nagel J. (2013). *Melodies of the Mind*. New York and Hove, East Sussex: Routledge.
Norman J. (2001). 'The psychoanalyst and the baby: a new look at work with infants'. *International Journal of Psychoanalysis*, 82: 83–100.
Norman J. (2004). 'Transformations of early infantile experiences: a 6-month-old in psychoanalysis'. *International Journal of Psychoanalysis*, 85: 1103–1122.
Ogden, T. H. (1989a). *The Primitive Edge of Experience*. New York: Aronson.
Ogden, T. H. (1989b). 'On the concept of an autistic-contiguous position'. *International Journal of Psychoanalysis*, 70: 127–140.
Ogden T. H. (2014). 'Fear of breakdown and the unlived life'. *International Journal of Psychoanalysis*, 95: 205–223.
Osborne N. (2009) 'Towards a chronobiology of musical rhythm'. In Malloch S., Trevarthen C. (eds.), *Communicative Musicality: Exploring the Basis of Human Companionship*. Oxford: Oxford University Press.

Panksepp J., Trevarthen C. (2009). 'The neuroscience of emotion in music'. In Malloch S., Trevarthen C. (eds.), *Communicative Musicality: Exploring the Basis of Human Companionship*. Oxford: Oxford University Press.

Petrella F. (2004). 'Procedere in psicoanalisi: immagini, modelli e miti del processo'. 64ème Congrès des Psychanalystes de langue Française, Milan, ms.

Piaget J. (1945). *La formation du symbole chez l'enfant: imitation, jeux et rêve, image et représentation*. Neuchatel et Paris: Delachaux et Niestlé; trans. by C. Gattegno and F. M. Hodgson as *Play, Dreams and Imitation in Childhood*. New York: Norton, 1962.

Piaget J. (1947). *La psychologie de l'intelligence*. Paris: Armand Colin; trans. by M. Piercy and D. E. Berlyne as *The Psychology of Intelligence*. London: Routledge and Kegan Paul, 1951.

Pichon-Rivière E. (1971). *El proceso grupal. Del psicoanális a la psicología social*. Buenos Aires: Nueva Visión.

Pigozzi L. (2008). *A nuda voce. Vocalità, inconscio, sessualità*. Turin: Antigone.

Plato. *Laws*, VII, 790d–790e. In *Plato in Twelve Volumes*, trans. by R. G. Bury, Cambridge MA: Harvard University Press/ London: William Heinemann, 1967, 1968.

Reik T. (1948). *Listening with the Third Ear. The Inner Experience of a Psychoanalyst*. New York: Farrar, Straus.

Reinberg A. (1998). *Le Temps humain et les rythmes biologiques*. Paris: Éditions du Rocher.

Rose G. J. (1993). 'On form and feeling in music'. In Feder S., Karmel R. L., Pollok G. H. (eds.), *Psychoanalytic Explorations in Music*. Madison, CT: International Universities Press, 2nd series.

Rosolato G. (1985). *Eléments de l'interprétation*. Paris: Gallimard.

Salem P., Coelho N. Jr. (2011). 'The role of imitation in the constitution of psychic reality: The contemporary psychoanalytic perspective of Thomas Ogden'. *International Forum of Psychoanalysis*, 20, 3: 129–137.

Salomonsson, B. (2007). '"Talk to me baby, tell me what's the matter now." Semiotic and developmental perspectives on communication in psychoanalytic infant treatment'. *International Journal of Psychoanalysis*, 88, 1: 127–146.

Salomonsson B. (2011). 'The music of containment: addressing the participants in mother–infant psychoanalytic treatment'. *Infant Mental Health Journal*, 32, 6: 599–612.

Schoenberg A. (1975). 'New music, outmoded music, style and idea'. In Stein L. (ed.), *Style and Idea. Selected Writings of Arnold Schoenberg*. New York: St. Martins Press.

Schumann R. (1970). *La musica romantica*, Ronga L. (ed.). Turin: Einaudi.

Serra C. (2012). 'Voce'. In Vizzardelli S. Cimatti F. (eds.), *Filosofia della psicoanalisi*. Macerata: Quodlibet.

Shakespeare W. (1994). *The Oxford Shakespeare: The Complete Works*. Oxford: Oxford University Press.

Stern D. N. (1985). *The Interpersonal World of the Infant. A View from Psychoanalysis and Developmental Psychology*. London: Karnac Books.

Tarde G. (1890). *Les lois de l'imitation*. Paris: Editions Kimé, 1993.

Turner R., Ioannides A. A. (2009). 'Brain, music and musicality: inferences from neuroimaging'. In Malloch S., Trevarthen C. (eds.), *Communicative Musicality: Exploring the Basis of Human Companionship*. Oxford: Oxford University Press.

Tustin F. (1986). *Autistic Barriers in Neurotic Patients*. New Haven: Yale University Press.

Valdrè R. (2016). *La morte dentro la vita. Riflessioni psicoanalitiche sulla pulsione muta. La pulsione di morte nella teoria, nella clinica e nell'arte.* Turin: Rosenberg & Sellier.

Wallin N. L., Merker B., Brown S. (eds.). (2000). *The Origins of Music*. Cambridge, MA: The MIT Press.

Williams, P. (2001). *Bach: The Goldberg Variations*. Cambridge: Cambridge University Press.

Winnicott D. W. (2017). 'The location of the cultural experience' (1966). In Caldwell L. and Taylor Robinson H. (eds.), *The Collected Works of D. W. Winnicott*. Oxford: Oxford University Press, 2017, VII, pp. 429–436.

Winnicott D. W. (1989). 'Fear of breakdown' (1974). In Winnicott C., Shepherd R. and, Davis M. (eds), *Psychoanalytical Explorations*. Cambridge, MA: Harvard University Press, 1989, pp. 87–95.

Zaltzman N. (1999). 'La pulsion anarchiste' (1979). In Zaltzman N. (ed.), *De la guérison psychanalytique*. Paris: PUF, 1999.

Index

Absence: 1, 3–5, 14, 15, 17, 21, 22, 24, 29–32, 35, 36, 52, 53, 55, 59, 61, 63, 64, 69, 72, 75, 79, 81, 82, 84, 88, 92, 99, 106, 110–118; of representation: 64
Accelerando: 100
Accent: 23, 30, 35, 73
Acoustemology: 1, 9, 10
Acoustic: 1, 7, 20, 25, 28, 65, 104; ecology and anthropology: 9; image: 8; impressions: 90; root: 98; sensibility: 12; sensoriality: 98; space: 90; *umbilical cord*: 89
Actualization: 80, 84
Adhesive equation: 54; *identification*: 54
Affect: 13, 20, 24, 26, 38, 41, 48, 62, 63, 67, 76, 84, 88, 92, 94, 98, 105, 108, 109, 113
Affective: 2, 82, 88, 92, 93, 114; dynamics: 93; experience: 15, 29; meaning: 13, 66, 94; motor: 66; semantics: 9; states: 66
Affiliative mechanisms: 10
Alienness: 50
Alpha function: 15, 32
Alterity: 32, 43, 65, 67, 78, 79, 83, 100, 105
Amnesic memory: 80
Analytic communication: 18; couple: 18, 114; group: 107; listening: 4, 68; process: 4, 5, 16, 118; relationship: 5, 15, 115, 117, 118; setting: 4, 38, 98, 113; situation: 71, 106, 118; work: 7, 18, 71, 111, 113
Anarchic drive: 52, 99
Anticipation: 4, 11, 19, 32, 33, 52, 53
Anticipatory annunciation: 73

Anxiety: 18, 43, 53, 54, 64, 74, 81, 84, 94, 102, 103, 110
Après-coup or afterwardness: 4, 15, 22, 32, 33, 49, 72, 80, 94, 100, 111
Archaeological metaphor: 71; model: 85
Archaic: 8, 49, 84, 108; atemporality: 94; unity: 83; time: 72
A-semantic language: 1, 12
Asymmetry: 27, 57, 107
Atemporality: 15, 94, 100
Atonality: 65
At-one-ment: 53
Audio-phonic skin: 27, 86
Audiovisual mirror neurons: 88
Auditive: 61, 92, 108, 115; ability: 100
Auditory: 1, 2, 3, 24, 94; ability: 5, 38; experiences: 89; representation: 41
Autistic-contiguous organization: 54, 88; *position*: 43, 54

Babbling: 35, 91, 93
Basic mental organization: 97
Beat: 10, 23, 25, 27, 39, 95
Being one: 32, 73
Bidirectional: 99; boundary: 90
Bidirectionality: 28, 72, 90, 99, 100
Binary logics: 21; structure: 4, 57, 100
Biomusicology: 3
Bodily: 29, 37, 86, 88, 107, 115, 117; change: 55; experience: 54, 117; memories: 117; motion: 89, 109; sounds: 18
Body: 4, 5, 11, 13, 20, 21, 29, 30, 32, 36, 39, 40, 58, 63, 65, 69, 73, 86–89, 92, 98,

99, 101, 108, 112, 115, 117, 118; experience: 99; image: 27; language: 98; position: 28; rhythm: 28; sound: 42, 90, 114; substance: 107; surface: 43, 60, 102
Border: 13, 34, 39, 55, 58, 63, 95, 96, 106
Boundary: 13, 28, 60, 85, 89, 90, 107
Break: 18, 21, 30, 81, 101, 106
Breath: 18, 26, 64, 114
Breathing: 40, 63, 69, 109, 111
Bruissement familial: 90, 112

Canon: 56, 57, 58
Capacity to be alone: 32, 85, 108
Castration: 85
Causal relationship: 60, 81
Chance: 21, 60
Chaos: 16, 53, 91
Chord: 23, 31, 45, 56, 64–67, 70, 98, 99
Chromatic fourth: 67, 68
Chronological time: 21, 60
Coaction to repeat: 51, 63, 81
Communication: 2, 3, 9, 10, 11, 18, 24, 27, 34, 35, 69, 71, 86, 102, 108, 110, 112, 116
Communicative function: 103, 108
Compromised message: 42, 62
Conceptual memories: 60
Condensation: 117
Conflict: 33, 85, 102, 103, 105, 113
Confusion: 35, 91, 99, 102, 105; of generations: 107
Conscious: 1, 4, 14, 22, 30, 32; representations: 1, 4, 98
Conscious-preconscious system: 32
Consciousness: 32
Consonance: 3, 26, 48, 64, 87
Consonant: 100
Contact: 9, 10, 17, 18, 28, 38, 50, 54, 60, 69, 94, 98, 111, 113
Container: 20, 48, 53, 102
Containment: 3, 15, 16
Contemporary music: 23, 52
Continuity: 4, 14, 18, 20, 21, 30, 42, 52, 61, 64, 78–80, 85, 86, 114; /discontinuity: 15, 88; *of being*: 20, 61
Contrapuntal: 57, 65
Corona: 30–32, 38, 92
Coronavirus pandemic: 24, 110
Cosmic time: 21, 60
Countertransference: 34, 38, 39
Co-vibration: 67

Creative acts: 92; gesture: 56; life: 48; processes: 58
Creativity: 43, 82
Crescendo: 87
Crying: 27, 28, 35, 89, 91, 113, 117
Culture: 7, 8, 9, 43, 86, 93

Dance: 7, 9, 57, 86
Death: 1, 7, 17, 22, 71, 72, 78, 81, 85, 94, 97, 113; anxieties: 83, 103, 104; drive: 52, 63, 66, 99, 100
Defence: 2, 34, 54, 62, 71, 84, 102, 104
Deferred imitation: 53
Deformation: 32, 51, 90, 91
Delay: 4, 31, 81, 82
Demarcation signifier: 90
Denial: 62, 63, 80; of time: 15
Depression: 74, 76, 79, 80, 81, 83, 84, 90
Depressive position: 43, 54
Descendent interval: 66
De-signification: 5, 69, 106
De-signified signifier: 42, 59, 62; word: 95
De-signifying listening: 5, 69
Desire: 15, 21, 33, 39, 59, 62, 72, 115
Developing variation: 52
Development: 2, 4, 6, 11, 15, 17, 19, 24, 26, 32, 35, 37, 39, 49, 50, 55, 57, 64, 66, 73, 100, 101, 116
Diachronic: 42, 73, 82
Diachronically: 64
Differentiation: 13, 39, 42, 55, 88, 90, 108, 117
Diminuendo: 87
Disavowal: 62
Discontinuity: 4, 21, 28, 33, 35, 61, 64, 82, 86, 87, 89, 100, 108
Discontinuous: 4, 15, 22, 49, 60, 72
Discretization: 27
Discrimination: 87, 90
Disillusion: 108
Dislocation: 34, 39, 42
Disobjectalizing function: 63
Displacement: 117
Dissonance: 3, 26, 52, 64, 65, 87
Dissonant: 12, 90, 100
Dodecaphonic: 65
Dream: 15, 72, 103, 106, 113–117; work: 113
Dreaming state: 91
Drive: 4, 15, 19, 32, 51, 62, 92; excess: 63, 103; *source-object*: 60, 62

Dyadic membrane: 107
Dyschronic: 36, 79, 108
Dyschrony: 34, 39, 85
Dysrhythmia: 109

Echo: 29, 93, 101, 112
Echoing: 90
Ego: 23, 30, 31, 33, 38, 51–53, 58, 60, 62, 64, 65, 86, 96, 102; boundaries: 55; defences: 2; functions: 51; identity: 94; skin: 4, 43, 102
Embodied simulation: 12
Emotion: 2, 10, 13, 14, 17, 26, 29, 30, 35, 42, 48, 49, 66, 82, 98, 104, 110, 111, 117
Emotional experience: 53; life: 59; state: 3, 48; tension: 53
Empathic understanding: 95
Empathy: 12
Emptiness: 14, 16, 17, 21, 22, 30, 82, 94
Empty signifier: 13, 59
Encounter: 5, 23, 25, 35, 53, 55, 58, 63, 69, 88, 117, 118; with the other: 98
Enigmatic message: 32, 42; Signifier: 48
Entrainment: 10
Envelope: 14, 18, 34, 39, 102, 111, 117
Epistemological solipsism: 11
Es: 30, 51
Étrangeté: 66
Event: 13, 21, 22, 24, 34, 39, 60, 61, 72, 80, 92, 107
Evolutionary musicology: 3, 9
Excess: 38, 61, 62, 63, 100, 103, 104, 106; of excitation: 62
Expectation: 3, 12, 14, 18, 19, 21, 26, 30, 31, 33, 35, 36, 38, 50, 57, 59, 61, 63, 64, 78, 79, 87, 92, 104, 109, 115
Experience of space and time: 101
External reality: 27, 49; stimuli: 11, 41, 53, 86; world: 20, 22, 29, 34, 61, 87, 90, 113, 115

False-self: 54
Familial environment: 116; rustling: 90; soundtrack: 90
Family: 4, 15, 17, 18, 19, 29, 37, 71, 73–76, 78–85, 90, 91, 101–107, 110, 115; environment: 90, 95, 97; group: 78, 83, 85, 89, 90, 101, 108; history: 74, 79, 81, 82; inter-rhythmicity: 108; music: 90, 104; setting: 82, 101; sound envelope: 103; soundtrack: 112; sound world: 90; structure: 109; temporality: 108; time and space organization: 83; unconscious: 107, 109; *vocal group*: 90, 91, 101; work: 82, 83, 106
Fear of breakdown: 38
Feeling-signs: 60
Fermata: 32, 115
Figurability: 101, 117
Fluctuating attention: 15
Foetal life: 3, 32
Foetus: 3, 20, 58, 87, 89–91, 108
Forclusion: 62
Formal qualities: 26, 87
Formal signifier: 13, 42, 59, 60
Formless: 54, 61, 106, 113; anxiety: 43
Found-created: 23, 52, 105
Fragmentation: 43, 88, 101, 102
Frequency: 19, 28, 30, 65, 100
Fundamental anthropological situation: 89
Fundamental note/sound: 65, 107
Fusion: 38, 52, 54, 93, 118
Fusionality: 100
Future: 15, 23, 30, 32, 36, 49, 63, 72, 79, 83, 89, 90, 92, 94, 107–109

Gap: 8, 15, 18, 22, 34, 35, 38, 43, 60, 62, 66, 67, 74, 79, 80, 84, 104
Gaze: 8, 17, 37, 74, 86, 98, 112
Gestural: 88, 92, 101; expression: 35, 88
Gesture: 9, 32, 40, 48, 56, 61, 97
Going on being: 11, 21
Group: 9, 10, 11, 38, 50, 57, 62, 65, 66, 71, 73, 78, 79, 85, 89–91, 93, 101, 105–109; *achrony*: 84, 108; dimension: 85; temporality: 85; time: 79, 108
Groupal illusion: 108; organization: 108; rhythm: 107; structure: 95; unconscious: 71
Guttural sound: 94

Hallucinatory phenomena: 69; states: 15
Harmonic: 21, 45, 56, 57, 64, 65, 70, 95, 108
Harmonics: 65
Harmonization: 50
Harmony: 4, 10, 30, 39, 42, 52, 56, 65–67, 91, 95, 99
Hearing: 8, 18, 35, 87, 94, 98; apparatus: 27, 87; sense: 87, 99
Heartbeat: 20, 28, 40, 91
Helplessness: 89

Hemisphere: 28
Heterochronic: 79, 108
Heterophony: 90, 91
Heterorhythmicity: 90
Historical time: 32
Historicizable: 61
Historicization: 61, 72, 79, 108
Historicized time: 72
History: 7, 33, 56, 57, 71–74, 78–82, 85, 108, 109
Hominization: 3, 7
Homophony: 91
Human evolution: 66; temporalization: 32, 78; voice: 26, 87, 104, 111
Hypnotic: 93

Id: 42
Idealization: 106; of the father: 19
Identification: 4, 8, 24, 35, 48, 49, 63, 65
Identity: 10, 33, 37, 79, 81, 91, 93, 94, 97, 99, 102, 104
Imitation: 4, 9, 12, 41, 48, 49, 53–58, 65, 93, 94, 99, 100
Imitative: 22; Functioning: 58; *process*: 55
Immemorial trace: 60
Immobilization of time: 84
Improvisation: 52, 55, 93
In-between: 59, 66, 67, 95, 98
Individuation: 85
Infans: 27, 32, 62, 101
Infant: 3–5, 10, 26, 27, 29, 36–40, 42, 43, 53, 54, 56, 66, 72, 86, 88, 89, 91–94, 96, 101, 103, 107; psychoanalysis: 3; research: 87, 92
Infantile: 118; fixations: 15; sexual: 5, 69; sexuality: 12, 23, 63
Infra-linguistic: 35
Infra-verbal: 14, 101
Inner world: 8, 14, 33, 36, 41
Intentional consonance: 12
Interaction: 10, 71, 90, 101
Intergenerational: 71
Intermediate time: 94
Internal perception: 22, 90; *imitation*: 12
Interoceptive sensation: 117
Interphantasmatic: 101
Interpreter function: 38
Interpretation: 10, 12–14, 18, 66, 72, 93, 95, 101
Interpretative work: 15
Interpsychic: 101

Interruption: 17, 19, 20, 101, 111
Inter-rhythmicity: 79, 108
Intersubjective: 5, 93, 98, 110; core: 99; dimension: 85; links: 85; origin of the psyche: 88; of the unconscious: 89; relationships: 108; structure: 109; temporality: 79; time: 118; unconscious: 71
Intersubjectivity: 37, 91, 95, 117
Interval: 5, 20, 45, 55, 57, 58, 65–67, 70, 95, 98, 99, 108, 116
Intimacy: 59, 60, 63, 66–68
Intimate: 59, 65, 69, 107, 110; stranger: 95
Intonation: 4, 17, 28, 29, 90, 91
Intrapsychic: 101
Intrauterine life: 27, 61, 89, 91
Introjection: 8, 54, 58, 92
Intrusion: 90
Irruption: 12, 18, 24, 116
Isomorphic: 3, 13, 21, 62
Isomorphism: 2, 5, 41

Judgement of attribution: 63
Judgement of existence: 58, 63

Key: 45, 50, 55, 65, 66
Kinaesthetic: 10, 61, 99

Lament bass: 67
Lament cry: 66
Language: 1–4, 6, 9–14, 20, 24, 25, 27–29, 33, 37, 39, 40, 42, 46, 48, 56, 64, 66, 69, 75, 77, 88, 89, 95, 96, 98, 100, 101, 104, 109, 117; evolution: 26, 66, 88; of music: 12, 13, 49, 88
Libido: 61
Life drive: 99
Link: 8, 9, 11, 18, 24, 26–28, 48, 49, 52, 54, 55, 61, 63, 66, 68, 71, 82, 85, 89, 91, 93, 108
Linking: 4, 5, 15, 37, 52, 64, 66, 69, 81, 92, 99, 100
Listener: 5, 28, 33, 49, 50, 55, 57, 63, 69, 100, 110
Listening: 1, 2, 4, 5, 8, 11, 14, 26, 28, 30, 37–39, 48–50, 52, 53, 57, 68, 69, 80, 87, 91, 94, 95, 98–100, 105, 109, 110, 111; to the self and the other: 96
Lockdown: 110
Loss: 17, 53, 61, 63, 84, 91, 94, 102, 116

Lost object: 29, 61
Love: 26, 37, 38, 52, 59, 62, 66, 90, 109
Lullabies: 91, 93

Maternal voice: 20, 21
Meaning: 2, 5, 8, 10, 11, 13, 14, 21, 23, 24, 26, 29, 30, 32, 35, 46, 48, 50, 51, 53, 56, 59, 63, 64, 66, 73, 78, 91, 93, 94, 98–100, 102, 104, 106, 109, 116
Meiosis: 79
Melodic motion: 18; profile: 90; superstructure: 27
Melody: 3, 4, 7, 9, 29, 30, 37, 39, 45, 49, 52, 55, 57, 58, 66, 69, 70, 93, 95, 98
Memory: 5, 14, 16, 19, 20, 23, 29, 33, 49, 50, 51, 55, 61, 63, 80, 81, 87, 92, 94, 103, 105; traces: 4, 41
Mimesis: 48
Minimal music: 50
Minor key: 65, 66
Mirror: 27, 50, 94; neurons: 88; stage: 86
Mirroring: 27, 28, 86, 87
Mnestic gaps: 15; recovery: 14; trace: 21, 47, 94, 117
Modulation: 50, 65, 91, 100
Monodic: 95
Mother-baby exchange: 4, 61
Mother's function: 60; gaze: 17, 86; voice: 3, 20, 21, 52, 87
Mother-infant body: 101; bond: 3, 6, 39; relationship: 3, 66, 86, 96; skin: 102; tie: 38
Motherese: 37, 92, 93
Motion: 3, 26, 32, 35, 37, 38, 45, 48, 50, 59, 61, 64, 66, 85–88, 90–93, 100–102, 108, 116, 117, 118; shape: 100
Motor development: 55; -gestural organization: 88
Mourning: 4, 5, 14, 15, 32, 33, 60, 61, 80, 83, 87, 94, 96, 99, 100, 115, 117, 118
Movement: 2–5, 10, 11, 13, 18, 19, 22, 28–30, 32, 33, 39, 41, 43, 50, 57, 59, 61, 64, 69, 73, 78, 86–89, 92–94, 98–100, 104–108, 110, 111, 114–116
Multidirectionality: 95
Music of families: 97; of the setting: 116
Music/noise splitting: 90
Musical competence: 28, 101; development: 57; dialogues: 86; discourse: 55, 64, 100; dynamics: 41; element: 14, 29, 30, 92, 100; experience: 2, 14, 26, 88; expression: 12, 48; form: 52, 56, 58, 107; functioning: 29, 57; instrument: 63, 92; language: 42, 49, 88; listening: 5, 69; object: 69; other: 40, 88; perception: 48; phrase: 24, 30; phrasing: 109; playing: 92; production: 50; relationship: 87, 96; sense: 99; style: 58, 100; structure: 3, 5, 26, 42, 108; symbolism: 100; syntax: 88; unconscious: 97, 101, 107, 109; *weaning*: 89, 95
Musicality: 26, 27, 37, 91
Musicotherapy: 2, 99
Musilanguage: 10, 26
Mutual adjustment: 93; exchange: 4, 61; gaze: 98; links: 82; reference: 95; relatedness: 1; tension: 73
Mutuality: 37, 88, 92, 93
Myth: 7, 10, 78, 84, 93
Mythical time: 82

Nachträglich: 72
Nachträglichkeit: 22, 72
Name: 36–38, 40, 77
Nameless terror: 32; /shapeless dreads: 103
Narcissistic contract: 93; envelope: 102; reparation: 33
Nebenmensch: 89
Negation: 22, 58, 62, 64, 81
Negative: 4, 38, 42, 58, 59, 61–65, 72, 81, 82, 84, 87, 99; affects: 76; hallucination: 35; listening: 5, 68; of perversion: 62; transmission: 73
Neoteny: 10
Neuroimaging: 28, 88
Newborn: 4, 9, 10, 16, 20, 27–29, 32, 87–90, 93, 94, 96, 107, 108; psychoanalysis: 95; scream: 89
Noise: 5, 8, 18, 20, 28, 34, 35, 37, 42, 64, 86, 90, 91, 97, 99, 101, 102, 104–109, 111, 112, 114, 117
Non-discoursive symbolism: 100
Nostalgia: 79, 87, 96, 100
Not-me: 63, 93, 95
Not-self: 28, 89
Nothing: 63
No-thing: 63
Nursery rhymes: 91, 93

Nurturing environment: 90, 109

O: 53
Object: 1, 3, 5, 13, 14, 20, 25, 26, 28–30, 33, 37, 42, 53–55, 58, 60–63, 65, 66, 69, 71, 79, 81, 84, 85, 87, 88, 98, 102, 104, 107, 113; absence: 32, 59; relatedness: 54; relationship: 54, 71
Obsessive defences: 34
Oceanic feeling: 2
Oedipus complex: 42
Off-beat: 25, 95
Olfactory envelope: 18
Omnipotence: 34, 36, 108
On-beat: 25, 95
Opposition signifier/signified: 3, 59
Original oneness: 91
Originary process: 58
Origins of life: 20; of music: 4, 9, 20; of psychic life: 3, 5, 19, 26, 35, 68, 88, 89
Other: 1, 4, 11, 17, 18, 22, 26, 28, 29, 32–34, 36–38, 40, 41, 43, 48, 53, 55, 58, 59, 61, 69, 73, 78, 79, 82, 85, 87, 88, 89, 92–94, 96, 98–102, 112, 116
Otherness: 5, 41, 43, 48, 52, 55, 58, 60, 79
Out-of-setting: 116
Outer world: 60

P-C system: 60, 62
Pandemic: 24, 110, 111, 118
Paranoid-schizoid position: 43, 54, 88; processes: 90
Parent: 16, 18, 19, 33, 34, 36–38, 73, 74, 77, 79, 82, 83, 84, 86, 87, 89, 102–107, 109, 111, 116; -child communication: 9; -infant dyad: 86
Parental bond: 11; figures: 48; function: 103, 107; identity: 34, 37, 93
Parenting: 36
Past: 23, 30, 32, 49, 51, 63, 64, 72, 79, 94, 108
Patient-analyst relationship: 66, 111
Pause: 18, 19, 20, 23, 30–32, 35, 45, 60, 63, 92, 115
Perception: 1, 4, 8, 14, 17, 18, 22, 28, 32, 39, 42, 49, 54, 55, 60, 62, 87–90, 94, 100, 101, 105, 114, 117; of distance: 113; signs: 4
Perceptive inscriptions: 60; signs: 60; traces: 60
Performer: 29, 31, 49, 56, 57, 63, 69
Permanence: 21, 72

Phantasy: 4, 32, 81, 83, 84, 94, 102, 103
Phenomenological time: 60
Phobic avoidance: 104
Phonic component: 94, 107; playing: 92
Phonological: 37
Phrasing: 18, 63, 109
Physiological rhythm: 93
Pictogram: 58, 60
Pitch: 29, 35, 39, 42, 70, 90
Play: 12, 13, 25, 49, 50, 52, 56, 57, 65–67, 77, 92, 110
Player: 13
Playing: 12, 14, 26, 34, 36, 65, 92, 96, 110, 114
Pleasure: 21, 50, 58, 65, 90–92; Principle: 22, 51, 52
Plural: 91, 95, 96, 98
Plurisubjective boundary: 90; links: 91; whole: 107
Poetry: 3, 4, 7, 9, 48, 52
Polymorphous: 63
Polyphonic: 55, 91, 95, 98, 107
Poliphony: 91
Pop music: 55
Positivization: 62
Potential space: 5, 54, 106
Preconscious: 22, 32, 48, 98
Predictability: 52
Prelinguistic: 35
Prelude: 31, 65
Prenatal experience: 41; life: 2, 5, 21, 58, 87, 89, 100; proto-object: 3; reminiscences: 20, 87; unit: 39
Pre-representational: 12
Presence: 1–3, 14, 16, 18, 20, 32, 33–36, 40, 53, 55, 63, 69, 75, 79, 80, 88, 92, 94, 100, 112, 113; /absence: 3, 21, 61, 79, 81, 88
Presentational symbolism: 100
Pre-subject temporality: 85
Pre-symbolic: 14, 42, 54, 55, 97, 102, 117
Preverbal communication: 13, 21; mnestic traces: 117
Primacy of the other: 43
Primal experiences: 2, 26; narcissism: 32; phantasies: 15; functioning: 38, 41; language: 89, 100; process: 38, 39; psychic activity: 98; relationship: 26, 27, 37, 103; repression: 42; rhythm: 34, 61; scene: 23, 102; semantics: 26; sensory experiences: 6

Primary communication: 86; defences: 62; dreams: 117; environment: 84; object: 54, 81, 85; processes: 5, 72; relationship: 87, 93; self: 58; sound: 91

Primitive: 5, 37, 41, 49, 53, 69, 90, 117, 118; agonies: 38; *edge of* experience: 42, 88

Primordial psyche: 4, 21

Principle of *difference*: 21, 57, 87

Projection: 33, 37, 54

Proper name: 37, 38

Proprioceptive: 28, 87, 94, 99, 108, 117

Prosodic: 37

Prosody: 18, 93, 107

Protective function: 62; screen: 18, 83; shield: 60

Proto-symbolization: 20

Psyche: 2–6, 13, 14, 20, 21, 23, 24, 26, 35, 37, 38, 41, 49, 55, 57–60, 62, 68, 71, 87, 88, 100, 101, 103, 118

Psychic activity: 1, 2, 30, 54, 68, 87, 89, 97, 98; apparatus: 60, 73; areas: 69, 85, 94; birth: 35, 98; borders: 55, 81; content: 47, 102; deformation: 32; development: 37; elaboration: 28, 62; envelope: 108; experience: 89, 100; functioning: 6, 29, 32, 41, 50, 61, 63, 73, 85, 99, 101, 108; life: 2–5, 7, 12, 19, 33, 37, 41, 43, 47, 59, 62, 64, 68, 88, 96, 98–100, 118; meaning: 98; motion: 5, 35, 37; movement: 69; organization: 97; process: 68, 72, 100; representation: 39; *skin*: 54, 69; space: 27, 84, 89, 108; structuring: 7, 32, 39, 41; surface: 66; time: 72; transmission: 4; work: 4, 19, 43, 48, 50, 53, 62, 80, 84, 90, 96, 99, 100, 111, 113, 117, 118

Psychoanalytic communicating: 110; listening: 5, 69, 94, 110; method: 71, 85; process: 15; situation: 12, 118; theory: 15, 62; work: 7, 111

Psychosensory functioning: 97

Pulsional excitation: 62

Reality: 8, 26, 27, 29, 33, 35, 48, 49, 60, 96, 104, 113, 117; index: 62

Reciprocity: 54

Recollection: 20, 49, 117

Referential language: 10; meaning: 10

Referentiality: 37

Regredient: 69; listening: 109

Regression: 4, 15, 72

Re-inscription: 47

Rejection: 34, 80

Relatedness: 1, 6, 54

Relational: 1, 8, 9, 32, 110; capacities: 11

Relationality: 73, 107

Relationship: 1–5, 9–12, 15–18, 20, 21, 26–28, 34, 36–39, 41, 44, 49, 54, 59–61, 65–67, 69, 71, 73, 74, 80–82, 85–87, 91–96, 98, 99, 102, 106–108, 110, 111, 115, 117, 118

Relinking: 64

Remembering: 49, 51, 71

Remote analysis: 112, 113; counselling: 118; session: 114

Reparation: 33

Repeating: 49, 53, 72

Repetition: 17, 19–21, 24, 30, 36, 41, 48–53, 55, 57, 60, 72, 81, 85, 92–94, 99, 116; coaction: 64, 81; compulsion: 51, 52, 92

Representation: 1, 2, 4, 7, 9, 19, 22–24, 30, 32, 34, 38, 39, 41, 42, 51, 53, 58, 60, 62, 64, 66, 84, 87, 98, 102, 113

Representational activity: 5, 32; functions: 35; process: 36; unconscious: 12

Repression: 15, 42, 62, 63, 81, 117

Re-signification: 72

Resolution: 21, 32, 41, 87

Resonance: 12, 67, 94

Respiratory rhythm: 20

Rest: 3, 16, 26, 30, 63, 86

Retroactive reverberation: 73

Return of the same: 93

Reverberation: 73, 118

Reverie: 32, 90

Rhyme: 91, 118; specularity: 118

Rhythm: 1, 3–5, 7–10, 12, 15–26, 28–32, 34, 37–39, 43, 45, 49, 52, 59–61, 64, 66, 79, 80, 82, 83, 86, 88–91, 93, 95, 99–101, 106–110, 115, 118

Rhythmic: 4, 9, 10, 17, 20–22, 27, 30, 33, 37, 41, 43, 44, 49, 52, 56, 91, 92, 95, 100, 101, 108; experience: 3, 87, 99; -phonic games: 91; memories: 3, 87, 99; *present*: 30; structure: 32, 91; variation: 55, 56

Rhythmical experiences: 20; time: 20

Rocking: 93

Rupture: 4, 5, 34, 38, 39, 43, 57, 61, 64, 84, 88, 102, 104

Sameness: 41, 52, 58, 60
Scenic diphasism: 23
Scream: 89, 90, 97
Secondary dreams: 117; function of understanding: 27, 89; *violence*: 38
Selective advantage: 10, 66
Self: 26, 27, 28, 34, 36, 42, 54, 58, 86–89, 94, 96, 98, 102; -awareness: 26, 87; -experience: 88; -phantasizing: 109; -generation: 58; -generative phantasy: 81; -historization: 61, 72; -perception: 60
Semiotic: 27
Semitone: 65
Sense of self: 54; of time: 5, 32, 61; of touch, smell and taste: 112
Sensorial apparatus: 60; envelope: 111; experience: 8; perception: 115; pre-unconscious: 89; reality: 60; reflectivity: 92; surface: 54
Sensoriality: 42, 60, 87, 88, 98, 101, 109
Sensorimotor: 92, 108; organization: 108
Sensory background: 42, 111; channel: 43, 61; deprivation I 10; environment: 111; experience: 6, 29, 43, 54, 70, 88, 93, 107; floor: 42, 54; information: 10, 39; kernel: 95; memory: 70; organization: 5, 39; register: 97; skin: 103; structure: 94; traces: 4, 97
Separation: 34, 79, 84, 92, 94, 97, 102, 106, 113; between subject and object: 113
Setting: 4, 15, 17, 18, 28, 38, 71, 82, 83, 98, 101, 111–118
Sexual: 5, 9, 10, 23, 29, 40, 42, 69, 100; excess: 106; theories: 62; unconscious: 89
Sexuale: 63
Shattered time: 15, 72
Sight: 7, 8
Significant form: 3, 13, 42, 59, 69, 100
Signification: 5, 14, 67, 69, 72, 106
Signified: 3, 13, 42, 59, 104, 106
Signifier: 3, 8, 13, 21, 42, 48, 59, 60, 62, 90, 106
Signify: 4, 22, 27, 29, 87, 92, 96, 100
Silence: 3–5, 13, 14, 16, 17, 21, 23, 24, 26, 29, 30, 42, 49, 61, 63, 64, 69, 70, 80, 86, 92, 97, 98, 100, 101, 106, 109, 110, 114, 115, 117, 118

Singing: 7, 93, 95, 97, 110, 111, 114
Skin: 27, 39, 54, 69, 86, 88, 102, 103, 112
Skin-Ego: 43, 102
Skype: 84, 111, 112, 115, 116
Social bond: 11; environment: 78, 90; group: 9, 93
Somatic borders: 39, 55; experience: 89
Somato-psychic: 20; being: 5, 100; birth: 29; functioning: 41, 61; functions: 39; relationship: 85; trace: 38; work: 50
Somato-sensory system: 11
Sonata form: 50
Song: 1, 9, 45, 86, 93, 95, 106; -birds: 95
Sonorous: 27, 53; bath: 27; *object*: 87
Sound: 1–12, 14, 18–21, 24, 26–30, 32, 33, 35–37, 39–42, 48, 49, 59–61, 64, 65, 69, 86–101, 104, 106–108, 110–112, 114–118; art of,: 4, 29, 59; *bath*: 35, 86, 87, 101; *body*: 99, 108; cell: 24, 56; confusional state: 35; containment: 17; decoding: 88; *dialogue*: 87; discourse: 102; discrimination: 90; element: 19, 64, 104; envelope: 4, 14, 20, 28, 29, 86–88, 101, 103; environment: 9, 89, 110, 112; exchanges: 92; experience: 3, 64, 87, 89, 90; games: 93; identity: 91, 99; material: 94, 95; mirror: 27, 86; perception: 28, 88; production: 1, 4, 10, 11, 91, 98, 101; register: 67; relations: 90; saturation: 35; skin-self: 27; space: 27, 34, 89, 91, 93, 99, 101, 108, 114; stimuli: 53, 93; transmission: 95; void: 5, 35; waves: 28, 39, 108
Sound-musical envelope: 90, 108
Sound object: 3, 20, 58
Soundtrack: 24, 90, 112
Space: 4, 5, 13, 15, 17, 21, 25–30, 34, 35, 37–39, 54, 55, 59, 66, 71, 73, 78–80, 82–84, 85, 87, 89–95, 98, 99, 101, 103, 106–108, 110–112, 114–116; -auditory image: 89; definition: 107
Spatial dimension: 39, 85; process: 39
Spatial-auditory body image: 27
Spiral time: 22, 23
Splitting: 34, 36, 40, 43, 62, 72, 88, 90
Spoken shadow: 38
Spokesperson: 35, 82, 103, 114
Spontaneous gesture: 48, 61
Style: 2, 4, 24, 43, 44, 50, 52, 57, 58, 65, 86, 92, 99

Strangeness: 67, 95
Stranger: 66, 95
Structural negativity: 62
Subject: 1, 5, 8, 9, 15, 17, 22, 28, 29, 30, 32, 33, 37, 38, 40, 43, 46, 48, 53, 58, 59, 61, 62, 67, 69, 71–73, 79, 81, 84, 85, 88–91, 93, 95, 96, 98, 99, 102–105, 107, 109, 117, 118
Subjectivation: 6, 33, 35, 38, 79; process: 22, 23, 29, 32, 38, 85, 102, 104, 107
Subjective: 55, 61, 91, 92, 107; experience: 54, 72, 108; interpretation: 93; rhythm: 108; temporality: 29, 60, 73; time: 85, 92
Subjectivity: 5, 22, 29, 38, 44, 53–55, 58, 65, 81, 85, 94, 100
Sublimation: 63
Suicide: 17, 74, 80
Superego: 15
Surface: 42, 43, 54, 60, 63, 66, 69, 72, 84, 88, 98, 102, 104
Surprise: 2, 17, 19, 52, 53, 61, 95, 105
Symbiotic quality: 102
Symbol: 3, 13, 35, 59, 72; of union: 32, 72
Symbolic: 14, 27, 32, 42, 54, 55, 91, 92; forms: 13, 27; functions: 5, 6, 53, 100; time: 85, 108
Symbolization: 6, 19, 21, 27, 29, 30, 50, 61, 73, 92, 117
Symbolize: 59, 87
Symbolizing abilities: 27; agent: 96
Symmetry: 43, 57, 88, 111
Synchronic: 63, 64
Synchronically: 82, 108
Synchrony: 14

Tactile: 10, 11, 20, 28, 43, 61, 92, 108; excitation: 18; sensation: 24, 87; -sound envelope: 4, 29
Talking cure: 2, 11
Tempered scale: 65
Tempo: 44
Temporal: 4, 10, 13, 14, 22, 30, 71, 81, 84, 87, 109, 118; dimension: 51, 90, 117; discontinuity: 87; movement: 107; organization: 38, 82; processes: 21, 39; specularity: 20; structure: 21, 32, 38, 61, 100
Temporality: 4, 5, 15, 22, 29, 32, 35, 49, 55, 60, 61, 71, 73, 78, 79, 81, 82, 84, 85, 100, 103, 108

Temporalization: 15, 32, 38, 44, 61, 72, 78
Tension: 21, 22, 33, 41, 53, 60, 63, 73, 87, 105
Therapeutic function: 71; group: 106; relationship: 3, 16, 39, 71, 80, 107; situation: 104; work: 16, 83
Thing-like other: 43; presentations: 42, 43
Thing-presentations: 1, 42, 62, 98, 100
Third ear: 2; topic: 71
Thirdness: 79
Thought: 8, 14, 19, 31, 32, 35, 48, 62, 64, 74, 83, 117
Three-dimensionality: 8, 28, 52, 54, 114
Timbre: 4, 29, 39, 52, 55, 65, 69, 90, 99, 118
Timbric specificity: 108
Time: 3–5, 11–25, 27–30, 32–37, 39, 41, 42, 45, 48–53, 56, 59, 60, 61, 66, 71–73, 78–82, 84, 85, 89, 92, 94, 96, 98–101, 107–112, 115, 118; construction: 92; obliteration: 72, 80; organization: 83, 95, 100; processing: 112; representation: 60; without temporality: 85, 108
Timelessness: 4, 11, 15
Tonal: 10, 18, 20, 50, 59
Tonality: 108
Tone: 3, 19, 27, 29, 42, 70, 73, 86, 93, 97
Tonic: 50, 64; changes: 92; *dialogue*: 86
Topical model: 71
Touch: 29, 97, 112, 113
Transcription: 41, 43, 44, 46, 48, 72, 108
Transference: 4, 12, 18, 34, 38, 39, 107, 113
Transformation: 5, 14, 15, 22, 26, 32, 33, 50, 53, 71, 78, 80, 111, 117
Transformational function: 38, 44, 45
Transformative: 25, 33, 69, 85; experience: 96; language: 96; model: 85
Transgenerational: 27, 71, 84, 102; time: 73
Transitional function: 95; object: 63, 113; phenomenon: 30, 91, 96; process: 32, 72, 95; representations: 1; space: 35, 115, 116; time: 85, 94
Transitionality: 11
Translation: 4, 32, 42, 43, 46, 48, 60, 62, 72, 99
Transmission: 4, 24, 29, 43, 73, 85, 95

Transpersonal defences: 71
Trauma: 19, 72, 80, 81, 117
Traumatic: 2, 24, 51, 111, 117
Traumatolytic function: 117
Tree of time: 15, 73
True self: 48
Trust: 11

Ucrony: 85
Uncanniness: 111
Uncanny: 5, 49, 81, 95, 106, 115, 117
Unchangeabilty: 72, 92
Unconscious: 1–4, 6, 11, 12, 14, 15, 22, 29, 32, 38, 40, 42, 43, 47, 53, 60, 62, 69, 71–73, 89, 95, 97–101, 105, 107–109, 118; communication: 2; conflict: 113; derivative: 72, 112; functioning: 49, 68, 99; legacies: 85; link: 107; message: 101; movement: 2, 107; phantasy: 4, 112; psyche: 2, 101; structure: 42; temporality: 38; time: 72
Unconsummated symbol: 3, 13, 42, 59, 69
Undifferentiated: 2, 11, 14, 37, 118; time: 82
Undifferentiation: 39, 103
Unison: 12, 53, 56–58, 91
Unlinking: 4, 5, 52, 64, 66, 69, 99
Unpredictability: 52
Unrepresentability: 52
Unrepresentable: 80
Unrepresented: 50
Unsaturated symbol: 13, 59
Unspeakable: 100, 101, 105
Unthinkable: 32, 34, 101
Untranslatable: 100
Upbeat rhythm: 16, 25
Ur-semantics: 26
Ursprache: 89
Uterine environment: 87, 90

Variation: 10, 19, 41, 49, 52, 53, 55–57, 67, 68, 92, 93

Verbal communication: 110; discourse: 29, 91, 99, 102; exchange: 101; expression: 88, 103; language: 1, 3, 9, 98, 101; structure: 95
Vibration: 4, 8, 20, 28, 29, 60, 63, 67, 87, 94, 98
Vibratory: 5, 29, 87, 92, 108, 112
Videoconferencing platform: 111, 112, 116–118
Vinculo: 71
Vision: 66, 97, 112, 114, 117
Visual: 8, 10, 24, 38, 61, 64, 87, 89, 103, 113, 114; blank: 35; element: 7, 19; excitation: 18; images: 2, 98; mirroring: 27, 87; object: 28, 87; perception: 1, 94, 100; sensitivity: 5
Vocal: 2, 4, 9, 10, 55, 90, 91, 95; cords: 65, 98, 115; games: 93
Vocalization: 9, 10, 93
Voice: 1, 3–5, 8, 12, 17, 20, 21, 26, 28, 29, 34, 35, 37, 52, 55, 58, 68, 69, 73, 87, 90, 91, 93–95, 97, 99–101, 104–107, 111, 113–115, 118; organs: 87, 94
Void: 5, 17, 19, 22, 23, 30, 32, 33, 35, 38, 61, 63, 64, 70, 103

Wahrnehmungszeichen: 60, 72
Wait: 82, 117
Waiting time: 118
Word: 2, 4, 5, 8, 9, 11, 12, 14, 17–19, 26, 27, 29, 36, 38, 42, 47, 54, 69, 80, 89, 91, 93–95, 97, 101, 102, 104, 105–107, 118; presentation: 62, 101; representation: 1, 98, 101
Work of mourning: 4, 5, 61, 81, 83, 88, 96, 99, 100, 115, 117; *of music*: 53; of the negative: 4, 58, 61, 62, 64, 81, 83, 88, 99; of nostalgia: 88, 96, 100
Working through: 12, 19, 33, 41, 51, 72, 82, 111, 117